The Childless Witch

Camelia Elias

THE CHILDLESS WITCH

TREMBLING

DANCE

VOICE

ORACLE

GRACE

EyeCorner Press

The Childless Witch:
Trembling, Dance, Voice, Oracle, Grace
© Camelia Elias 2020.
Published by EyeCorner Press.
Designed and typeset by Camelia Elias.

ISBN: 978-87-92633-57-6
ISBN EBOOK: 978-87-92633-58-3
December 2020, Agger, Denmark

EYECORNERPRESS.COM

Come witches, come,
Come help me with the spell of death,
and the mourning after.

— WALPURGISNACHT, 2020

Images and Illustrations

Camelia Elias on the beach in Agger (14). Photo by Bent Sørensen. Camelia Elias and Zohar Fresco in Houdetsi (32). Photo by Miguel Hiroshi. Camelia Elias in Houdetsi (36). Photo by Ross Daly. Camelia Elias and Frigg (37). Photo by Bent Sørensen. A calligraphy series based on the butoh dance *Åy Amour* by Carlotta Ikeda and Ko Murobushi (41, 48, 50, 54) by Camelia Elias. Camelia Elias in butoh performances (63, 82). Jean Noblet Marseille Tarot as reconstructed by Jean-Claude Flornoy (96, 119) Reproduced here by kind permission from Roxanne Flornoy. Anonymous witch installation on the beach in Agger (108). Photo by Camelia Elias. Camelia Elias' parents, in private collection (129).

Contents

Prologue

WATER WAS RUNNING DOWN the neighbors' walls. We blamed it on the flowers. Every hot summer evening mother would take care of the flowers on our long balcony. Once mother was done spritzing her pots, it couldn't be helped that some of the water went running from our elevated apartment to the apartment below us. This was an old *Jugendstil* building in Romania we lived in, featuring two floors of apartments arranged around an inner square space. You couldn't make a move without others noticing it. It was not so with philosophy, metaphysical and wisdom questions. Those were blocked out by default by the neighbors. No one had time for crazy ideas. Except for us, three women living at the South end of the building. A widow and her two daughters. I was barely a teenager when I had the strange idea to ask mother a question one doesn't normally ask. As we sat there enjoying the breeze from the flowers that were doing their best to please us, I asked her: 'if you had one thing to give us, your greatest idea, what would it be?' She gave me a long look, yet answered unhesitatingly: 'don't have any children. You'll be the happier for it.' Whoa, I'm not sure I got the full implication of her statement, but I instantly took it to my heart.

My sister was not so quick in her acceptance. She retorted angrily: 'what a bizarre thing to say. You had us, what of it? Do you regret it?' My mother looked at her with some measure of disgust. Her trade was logic. She made an effort to pass logic on to us in all its manifestations, from the formal to the common. Which part of her statement did my sister not get? And why would she mix the narratives? What exactly could prevent a mother of two daughters to pass her best wisdom to them in the form of 'don't have any children?' Why wasn't this allowed? What would be the reason for it? A storm of gazes was forming and I knew that if I didn't intervene, the idyllic sitting on the porch with the flowers would be ruined. I turned to my sister, and before mother had a chance to ambush her with all sorts of weapons in the category of combating fallacies of affectations, I told her to keep silent, and think first.

I asked a question in earnest, and mother answered in earnest. What was there to judge? If my sister wanted to object, all she had to do was present mother with an argument, or ask her to explain. Mother liked both, arguments and to explain. Idiotic dismissals of what she said due to emotional overreactions were not welcome. But sister didn't want to object by offering an informed opinion. She preferred pouting. As she was also well versed in losing arguments against mother, she refrained from further showing her unsubstantiated disapproval. The excess water now reached the ground floor, and we heard no objections coming from there either. Forty years down the road I'm still childless. Sister not so. She is a mother. She got revenge for her silenced attitude, but what of that evening's wisdom?

Although I told this story on a number of occasions, not once did I say to anyone who asked me why I don't have any children that it was because mother said it would be a bad idea. People expect you to argue, take a strong position, defend yourself. 'Mother said I shouldn't have any children and so I won't' is not the appropriate response. But why not? I've been interested in this ever since.

People take to their hearts what their parents say to them all the time, for better or worse, but when a mother tells her daughters, whom she loves, that they'd be better off without children in their lives, it's not acceptable. Most mothers would convince their daughters that there's power in motherhood. This is entirely normal, for what *can* they say that would be a valid experience of the state of childlessness? Mothers don't have the habit of imagining what power there may be in being a woman without children. They might imagine that there's less hassle and perpetual worrying that goes into it, but as far as experiencing the freedom connected to the state of childlessness, it would be safe to say that such an experience would be non-existent on the tangible plane. As a consequence, motherhood is pushed forward as a creative act *par excellence*, but this is a modern construction. Setting cultural symbolism aside, from a strictly anatomical perspective it's hard to see what is 'creative' about reproduction. What is creative is the story around the purpose of children, most of it associated with hope and a thinking forward about the future of humanity.

Hence, most daughters would have a similar reaction to my sister's, being unable to imagine how a mother could say to them not to procreate. But I think that what's more interesting is the inverse of the situation. Instead of saying, 'I can't even begin to imagine that she'd say that,' one *could* imagine what a childless life might look like in actuality. Surely a woman's purpose on this planet can't be measured solely according to standards of fertility or her willingness to live for no other reason than to have children.

For my part, I was in for the ride, not just to imagine myself as a childless woman, but to also act on it. As far the imagination is concerned, I also like to think about just what people might say, if I said this in my 'defense': 'I don't have any children because my mother, who was both a logician *and* a witch, said I shouldn't have any.' You want to bet that people would nod? 'Ah, yes, that explains it.' In my imaginary conversations about it, I always say, 'it explains what exactly? What does *it* refer to?' People would look helpless, would point to the witch and dismiss the logician, and I would be rolling on the floor. Just this scenario alone would be enough to make me decide once more, if I could go back in time, that, indeed, the childless existence is rather priceless.

'I know it's priceless, and I hate you,' my sister who actually loves me to bits and pieces once said, when we got very hot in a sauna together with another woman who was also childless. While I was steaming myself to dissolution, the two were talking about children. 'I regret that I didn't listen to mother,' my sister said, telling our friend the exact same story I'm recounting here. I opened one eye and looked at her in disbelief. She is the type who dotes on her son. She squinted at me, giving me also one eye to match the one I was giving her: 'don't give me this look', she said. 'You know, I *can* keep the narratives apart,' she then said. 'I *can* love my son, and still imagine that if I could choose again, I would choose to be childless.' 'Ha,' I wanted to say, reminding her of the other hot night years earlier, when mother suggested the same, but I refrained. The other childless woman in the room said: 'I'm not a witch. But I can predict when someone dies or when they divorce.'

We all looked at one another trembling with excitement, wishing to go out and dance, read cards, and sing. We were the three graces, all childless in thought and two also in physicality, seeing right through the wisdom of a clever mother, and receiving its gift for precisely what it was: excess water on the neighbors' walls, refreshing the world of conventions.

Of lamentation

WE COULD LAMENT MORE than the absence of children in the life and times of a woman, if the art of lamentation was still in fashion. Before she had children that she then murdered in an act of revenge against her moron lover, Euripides' Medea was a fine witch.[1] Before having her son, Isaac, the Biblical Sarah was a powerful witch whose word was obeyed on command. And it goes like this, all the way back to the story of the Garden of Eden, to Eve, who was also doing fine with being a knowledgeable woman, until she committed the *faux pas,* which was to share an apple with Adam, thus bringing God's wrath upon herself.[2] It's not written in the Bible in this tone, but since I have a vivid imagination, I can just see this different variation in which God yells at the witch: 'If you absolutely had to be so stupid and not really mind your own business and keep the stuff you discover to yourself, I must condemn you to a life of children, so you won't have time to eat magical fruits that will make your head pop like *abracadabra*, allowing you to initiate yourself in saying *Open Sesame!*'

Now, I don't go around telling this story to just about anyone, as I don't fancy the idea of being accused of discrimination, but I do like to think about why a childless woman simply can't stay that, childless, without others having an opinion about it. Given the treatment that women have received from patriarchal societies, which is to say, the whole world, it's not news to anyone that, just by being born a woman, one is a witch already, the seeds of disobedience already having been planted within her. By a cultural reversal, then, we can argue that a witch first becomes a woman when she agrees to sanction what is expected of her: sit in her bench, wait for him to come, not talk, and not touch his body. He will do the right thing – or not – and if she's lucky enough to get the ring – then all hell becomes respectable: here come the children, and with them the status. The witch who questions this consecrated womanhood is a bad witch, eradicating her right to enter *the proper*, in the sense also of eradicating her right to become the fine property of another.

Now that we're at it, and before we get ahead of ourselves, let us insert right here and right now our first definitions: *a witch is one who poses true questions. A childless witch is one who understands the business of self-reliance and acts in accordance with having answered a true question* – here I don't discriminate between the women who are childless by choice and by inability.

Asking a true question is another way of saying that one questions all social constructs from the position of being aware that the *I* asking the question is already beyond these social constructs. Embodying such a state has never been a good idea, culturally speaking, as it's the surest recipe for marginalization and persecution, but it *has* been beneficial to the one who understands the significance of acting out of singular expression, rather than collective belief. The witches that posed true questions and just stayed childless as a consequence, from myth to folklore to modern times, simply had one 'privilege' only: to hang, or get the door of their mouths closed.

Fast forward to the present day, when childless women with a high profile career, such as Tracy Emin, lament: 'They think I'm a witch, because I have deliberately stated that I've no interest in children'[3]. Since Emin is an artist, the easiest is to understand her statement as part of an art project, because what else is the alternative in this day and age of meaning, seeking meaning, selling and buying meaning, and creating meaning out of nothing, making others believe in it? That life has meaning because there are children in it is not something one can easily contest, unless one would like to point to what is wrong with the culture of success.

According to statistical evidence, if a childless woman says to someone, 'I don't have any children,' the suggestion that scores the highest in the department of solutions, even when none are sought, is the following: 'you can adopt.' This is all fine, if the inherent premise for this response would not, actually, be one of consumerism. I think that at least on one occasion I retorted back as a childless woman myself: 'yes, I could do that. After all, it's no different than putting a coin into a dispenser and have a child pop out of the machine. But what if I preferred another kind of entertainment?'

The age we live in is, indeed, no longer an age of lamentation. We lost that art long ago. In place of lamentation we now have success rates. Can we count being childless among our blessings? What of real laments? Can we bring them back? And are all laments in order, or equally powerful? There are many more things we can lament than the absence of children in our lives, and that includes lamenting the books that proliferate in both the academic and the mainstream market that purport to teach us how to be childless.[4]

In my own book here I want to look particularly at what makes a childless woman not only a powerful witch, according to standard definitions of the cultural stereotype, but also a woman able to cast a powerful spell of movement, a movement that goes from trembling to dance, to the use of voice, the oracle, and a state of grace.

In making a distinction between cultural perceptions of the woman who has no children — for whatever reason — and the understated affairs when the childless witch is forever the Other Woman, the antagonist of the figure of the mother, Lilith contra Eve — what we find is actually a discourse on love: 'how much? Just how much does he love me?' Culturally speaking, the mistress who is coerced into the state of not having children because the domain of procreating is reserved for the respectable wife, it's tempting to assume that while the mistress beholds the man's heart because of passion, the wife sits on the throne that spells it out for the community: 'this much' – the chin is raised, the gaze proud, the finger pointed to the elevated seat. Hillary Clinton multiplied. The wife of a president must fulfill her function as protector. 'But he loves me more,' the mistress wants to lament, and on occasion, when she turns to some very bad witchery, she goes to the media. Two women in love with the same man – or should we say, invested? – get busy: the wife hires a detective; the childless witch phones the paparazzi: 'on such and such a day, I'll make sure to have his private parts in just your viewfinder, while I myself will play innocent, yet, hot – or else, there's always that stained dress you can use for an impeachment.'

Sometimes the roles are not so clear, with the cultural order of things getting screwed up. In Euripides's story, it may well be that the grand witch Medea got to be enthroned as the wife, but she never managed to feel that role in her bones, remaining strangely the Other Woman. And yet history repeats itself or sets new records, with the antiquity's Medea sending off her magical familiars to spy on Jason, only to find out that he, as feared, was cheating on her. Oh, the drama, just like modern times. If only she could go back to her childless state. Which she did. To everyone's horror. Or *was* it really a horror, this tragedy filled with resentment and regret? We're here to investigate. Euripides's Medea is fascinating as it moves back and forth between the tale of the childless witch and the wife's tale.

What stays unmoved is the question: 'how much?' Armed with this obsession for precision, I propose that we take this question and look at a few women, both real and imagined, and go past the tedious cultural stereotype that merely casts the childless woman as a witch, a sorrowful bitch, or as a 'mother at heart, truly, who sadly cannot conceive'. I'm not sure why so much sadness must be involved in all this type of lamentation, what with speaking here from the position of a writer who practices Zen and martial arts cartomancy, but what I find infinitely more interesting to look at is what we can say about the power that a woman who has no children beholds, actually, beyond even the desired identity for identifications with inaccessible goddesses of love and war, because – sigh – what's the alternative?

Yes, the sigh. Yet not the sigh produced by the childless woman who is a mother at heart – truly – but the sigh that identifies a glimpse of power in the nothing that is. When men repudiate women with this line: 'you're nothing without your children,' I see that what they are actually doing is to pass judgment on the woman's highest state of being. But how many women realize this before they succumb to sadness? I'm interested in the women who do know the implications of 'you're nothing without your children,' and act in accordance: they dance, they tremble with desire, they issue the most frightening spells, they read signs with the precision of a rocket scientist, and they behold a state of beauty and grace, being balanced beyond mortal imagination.

I'm interested in how the women who are 'nothing without children' – except for their embodied power – can sing a whole requiem for other childless witches, who, like Medea however, became mothers for naught. What I'm *not* interested in is to tell a story of 'what could have been.' Medea paid for her transgression – going from being a powerful witch to being a pathetic mother – and that is enough. The better story is the story of celebration, not of rage, the story in which the childless witch doesn't lament the societal stigma around her predicament or choice.

When societies get very busy with suppressing the woman's trembling with desire, dance, voice, oracular power, and state of grace, they do so because they see that there's power in all this; power that's not negotiable; power that won't limit itself to any clubs. In this, I will advance the claim that the childless witch is one beyond identity games, sanctioning her own power as power, not as something that requires adjectival modification. There's no good witch and bad witch here, just a story about women who understand that they are not at anyone's mercy, especially not at the mercy of some fantasy children.

In my short selection of examples, I have deliberately picked both women and men artists, simply because it's easier to talk about their advantage in being childless without having to engage with identity politics. This being the case, what I have to offer here is not a history of the childless witch, nor a biography in fragments. What I offer instead is a reflection on how the witch as one who poses true questions is simply enough unto herself, and because she knows it, she stays childless, enjoying, if not all, then at least one of the states I want to discuss through personal stories, through the essayist mode of the memoir: trembling, dance, voice, oracle, grace.

Ultimately I may say that this is not even a book about women or a few good childless men, but rather about liminal states and the ones who dare to embody them in a sovereign and original, yet classic way. While saying *no* to cultural and societal forms of dictations can be an expression of sovereignty, saying *no* is not original, even when not very many dare to say it. But it *is* a classic, precisely because it's available to all, regardless of the positions one happens to entertain.

While I'm interested in the childless woman's *no* and her embodiment of the negative, this book is not a manifesto for anti-motherhood. Others before me did a good job already at depicting the childless woman as a witch in adversarial position to the more privileged concepts of the maiden and the mother, and anthropologist Margaret Meade's words about men and sorcerous women in Bali still resonate:

The figure of the witch who kills living things, who strokes the throats of children till they die, whose very glance causes cows to lose their calves and fresh milk to curdle as it stands, is a statement of human fear of what can be done to mankind by a woman who denies or is forced to deny childbearing, child-cherishing (Mead, 1949: 215)[5].

Here, I will simply discuss joy, the sheer joy associated with being free, being free of expectations and labels included. For, the first realization that the woman who poses questions from the heart makes is that there isn't the number of mirroring games she can play that can compete with the idea of being beyond identity and identifications. This is another way of saying that when a woman makes art of her life – which is the opposite of acquiring an identity – she 'witches' herself into a state of perpetual magic, where her childlessness is even beyond merely casting an enchantment unto herself in the popular form of what we call 'self-empowerment.' For instance, most of the self-empowerment encountered in self-help books is the result of taking personal offence at just about everything and everybody. I'm not interested in feeling as narrative, this kind of deeply feeling the world when both the world and the feeling are under the influence of the impressionable. The passion I'm interested in is the result of a careful calibration of what is actually the case.

At the practical level, I'm interested in extrapolating from the expressions of trembling, dance, voice, and the oracle, the grace that we call talismanic power, the power that we draw down from the moon, when we dare to both face it, and lose ourselves behind its face in darkness, our reason still intact and brilliant.

1   See *The Greek Plays: Sixteen Plays by Aeschylus, Sophocles, and Euripides* (Modern Library Classics, 2017).

2   See: 'Genesis 3:1-24,' *The Holy Bible: King James Version* (1611). (Cambridge Pure Edition, 2019).

3   'They think I'm a witch because I'm childless and have no desire to be a parent, says Emin at the opening of homecoming show.' Eleanor Harding for the *Daily Mail*. May 26. 2020. *Mail Online*. [https://www.dailymail.co.uk/news/article-2150196/They-think-Im-witch-Im-childless-desire-parent-says-Emin-opening-homecoming-show.html] Last accessed: June 11, 2020.

4   See for instance Rachel Chrastil's book: *How to Be Childless: A History and Philosophy of Life Without Children* (Oxford University Press, 2019).

5   See Margaret Meade's influential book *Male and Female.* (New York: Harper Collins, 1949). Since she first formulated her ideas about the concept of the witch in the 20s, Meade has been critiqued as a scholar and anthropologist, but one must give credit to her insightful reflections that are based on matter-of-fact, rather than interpretation.

Trembling

ℐ CAN'T STEP OUT OF THE HOUSE to meet another dog. My Husky/German Shepard mix, one that I like
to call Frigg, the she-dog goddess, has her own ideas as to
who and how we greet others. She is a dominant type who
fears only one other person on the planet: me. The minute
I welcomed her into my life, I had a close *tête-à-tête* with her
three-months furry existence. I said: 'you're young, which is
quite unfortunate as I have little patience for young ones, but
I'll try my best. What you need to know, however, is that I
don't negotiate.' 'Woof,' she said, and I decided that her response was one of complete understanding. Now she's eight
and as childless as myself. She's thinking about it, the puppy
thing, especially when a big dog comes around to sniff her.
She could have them on the spot, if I let her. But I tell her
to cut it out, her fantasy of offspring, as it's not something
we dig in our household. Frigg learned to mirror my prefer-

ences, and we never discuss why I always have to decide. If we're outside, we like to meet two types of other four-legged fellow beings: the obscenely fluffy ones whose ears go up in a *spitz* and puppies. Frigg is ever so excited at what I can only imagine is her imagination. But her excitement stops as soon as the other dogs seek my hand. I simply must not use my hand to touch any other dog. The sweetest puppies enjoying their puppy permit come close to being terminated on the spot, if they fancy making a pass at me. Frigg gets aggressive and barks in the same non-negotiating tone I bark at her. So I can never enjoy the pleasure of seducing other dogs while on her watch.

What I observe that I find interesting, however, is the trembling that goes into the frenzy of rejecting anyone aspiring to my hand. There's high determination in this trembling. The softest fluffs a minute ago can turn to pulp if they get the wrong idea. When trembling announces that we're now in the presence of a strong death resolve, what we see is not just the hair that rises, but how the whole body goes into a swaying that's geared towards precision. It's like going into a trance, yet one in which there's no distinction between drive, determination, and target. An aroused animal doesn't negotiate with its sense of precision.

In shamanic parlance, before the witch crosses the threshold into the realm of visions, she can experience trembling, loss of bodily control and composure.[1] The eyes get crossed and ready for distinctions that are not of the mundane world.

The sweet can turn bitter, the soft harsh, and the sharp can melt on the tongue. Magic. When Frigg goes into what she perceives is a combative mode of counter-attacking, the last thing on her mind is the possibility to adopt the puppy she's now ready to kill, leave a legacy, and be proud of making a difference in the world. Frigg is a goddess without cultural morals. Her spine is not made of morals. She just does what there's to do. She knows instinctively the difference between right and wrong. She is always right in protecting me. I heed attention to how she is in the world, and to how she navigates the sophistication of *non serviam*. You'd think that she takes her existential values from the other Frigg, the Norse goddess of wisdom, the quiet and often unidentifiable wife of the god everyone heard of, Odin. Frigg may have been the first lady, but she was no icon of her generation. She was a *völva*, a seeress, and a knower of all fates. She was a witch beyond trembling, yet instilling trembling fear in all who knew her – that includes her famed husband and her sons. Or so the legend goes, reporting also on how, in spite of being the goddess of marriage, in addition to wisdom, Frigg was not what you nowadays call 'faithful'. She sought other bellies to touch than that of her intended.[2]

Trembling stuff, indeed, to think that the one who could weave the clouds actually had the power to make others pop in and out of existence. This magical power is interesting to consider, especially in the context of motherhood. In her confession years ago, perhaps my sister was channeling this power, when, for a moment, she transported me and our friend to the land where motherhood deprogramming was possible. If either of us childless women ever flirted with the idea of becoming mothers, my sister's *ad hoc* magic made us snap out of it.

HEART OF A BELLY

Trembling makes the heart of a childless witch stop, in order to re-calibrate its pulse. As part of a series of rituals that involved Norse magic à la hedge sitting and *seidr* in both Denmark and Norway with reputed shaman and *völva* Anette Høst, I once also thought of going South. In 2011 I went to the island of Crete, though not to meet the Greek gods, but an Israeli devil in the incarnate form of drummer Zohar Fresco.

I've always been against the idea that life is something that one seizes, one grabs, and one adds to the list of things and achievements that one wishes to take into one's grave. Let's face it, life is something we experience, perhaps the way one experiences light, and it has nothing to do with what we make of it. This latter idea, of making something of life, is mainly an idiotic Western thought developed to counter both the fear of death and the feeling of guilt for not investing enough time and energy into thinking about what life really means. When I went to Crete I was fortunate to spend time among people who, for the most part, were trying to understand what life is on its own terms. The questions posed were simple: What is flow? How do we experience being in the now? Can we get naturally high through practices of fasting, breathing, and conscious exercise?

When asked about it they all said: 'everything is connected, so why bother with petty things and cultural constraints?' Most of these people didn't have families and children, they didn't do the right thing in terms of getting a solid and stolid job, and they didn't give a flying fuck about moral principles based on hypocrisy, lying, and regular dishonesty. They didn't negotiate with symbolic cultural values and they didn't compromise either. It was clear to me that they were the embodiment of the Romanian saying: 'if you can't get the stallion, don't settle for the mule.' They were all drummers attending a drumming workshop in Houdetsi organized by music director Ross Daly and the Labyrinth, featuring the best master, the Lord of the Frame Drums himself, Zohar Fresco – also the Lord of Light, what with his name, Zohar, translating into Splendor. He kept it simple too: 'remember that you're here to serve and to read souls.'

Listening to such words was like being in an archery competition where I was the target. As the arrows hit my spine, they made my body tremble. I looked at Zohar's eyes. His soul was made of fur. Being older than him I thought I had an edge where the reading of the soul is concerned. I tried to get a sense of his belly, but it was hidden behind his round frame drum. To penetrate through layers of skin requires special shamanic techniques that don't necessarily fall in the category of shamanism as an invention of the New Age movement.

I'm interested in the movements of the body, especially the subtle ones, but I find having to wait in order to perceive what's happening more fascinating, as this waiting places me in the empty space around a phenomenon, such as the experience of a speaking voice, or a black dot on a white page that calligraphers describe as negative. Social intelligence is defined by the ability to read an environment. I'd say that reading souls is defined by the ability to read negative space.

By virtue of his mysteriously enchanting capacity, one could argue that Zohar Fresco also falls in the category of witch. Childless too, last I've checked. This is a man who can induce trembling on command in anyone listening to him. He has not only mastered reproducing intricate patterns of rhythm, but he has also mastered the art of simplicity, elegance, and correspondence. He communicates through dynamic soundscapes made up of equal measures between four elements: pulse, color, energy, and spirit. In my encounter with him, he had this to say: 'the drum is only a tool, *tav* in Hebrew, and has embedded in its name both the idea of oneness and life. Then there is also the idea of connection – the Hebrew letter *vav* is the sound of being joined, one *and* another.'

I let myself be pulled into the kabbalistic philosophy of Zohar's drumming, and thought about how astonishing the idea of joining is, yet joining not horizontally, as one may think is more immediately logical, but vertically. Of course, the one and the other cannot and should not be dissolved into one another. They must remain independent. 'Before a child is born,' Zohar intoned: 'the first thing that he hears is his mother's pulse and her voice.' 'Remember,' he then said by turning to the majority of drumming men in the room, 'what we all want is this, to hear the woman's voice and her pulse. The woman always wins, remember that.' Zohar was now looking at me. The others followed his gaze. Something in his voice left no room for disagreeing. He spoke softly, and his words flew as did his fingers on the drum. I insisted on touching his hands for the whole time I was present. He let me, and we both felt the power of the *shekkinah*, the power of dwelling in the divine.

Scholar of Judaica and kabbalistic mysticism, Gershom Scholem, argued that the concept of the *shekkinah* as related to the woman, the divine feminine, is the most popular idea among the notions of the significance of that which arrives in mysterious ways, the Greek *parousia* for presence or, indeed, the arrival of the holy ghost, the dove, or a shattering power.[3]

This arrival should not be confused with the arrival of a child, as its force is of a different magnitude. When the *shekkinah* manifests as woman, she has the force of all the Pomba Giras of the world, in the Quimbanda lore, the Lord of Splendor's bride, Lucifer.[4] The Kabbalists would not be happy for this analogy, but since I have Zen inclinations, I don't ask for permissions. Zohar knew why I was there. I didn't have to tell him. He saw it for himself.

I ordered lamb entrails at the restaurant that we were eating at. He, a vegetarian dish. I had spirits and wine. He, plain water. While stuffing myself great gourmet style, I was philos-ophizing on the power of the *shekkinah*. I had just written a few academic papers on the erotic in this type of mysticism, so my head was full of it.

After the touching of hands part and the careful observance of Zohar's belly and breath, I had to replenish myself. I told him that I grew up in Romania eating entrails, and that it was hard to get any in Denmark, where I'd been living for three decades. I didn't tell him this as an excuse. I didn't have to, as this power food was already part of my own 'essentials,' moving forcefully through my arm, grabbing him.

So, was I in Crete to eat? Yes, I was there to eat sounds and vibrations. I wasn't there to imitate Zohar's inimitable style, nor was I there to learn how to drum. I was there for the light, the formless form, which yet in his hands exuded the rigor of discipline. He masters to perfection not only what can be turned into articulate and clear sound, but also the voiceless, what he calls the ghost notes. I liked those notes the best. They allowed me to follow the movement of his hand into *almost* sound. The sound of the silent O. 'I'm zero,' Zohar said, 'I start from zero on this round thing which is the drum, a zero itself, and I give nothing. But I want this nothing to move people.' His playing moved me. I cried. And then I cried some more as I realized that he played just for me. This was on our last night together. That is, together with twenty-two other childless witches. Most of them called themselves percussionists, but others didn't have a problem with the witch appellation. A certain tacit understanding regarding names informed our gathering.

After seven days of instructing us in the mystery of the frame drum, Zohar was treating the witches to a private concert. We had to ride into town for it. Those with cars gave a lift to those who didn't have a car. Along the way to the concert hall, the driver of our vehicle suggested that the five of us stopped in some bushes for a smoke. As I prefer the natural high to substances, I realized what was going to happen. We were going to miss half of Zohar's concert, if not all of it. I was not going to allow it. I had to step in and issue a command. 'Over my dead body are we going to stop anywhere. We're late already,' I said. 'We will make our arrival on the dot. I have to sit in the front row parquet,' I then said adamantly and very explicitly. The other four in the car gave me a sheepish look. 'If you insist,' they said. I insisted. We made it on time. I sat right across the musicians, and under Zohar's nose.

From my vantage point I had an excellent view of his belly. It was moving in the right way. After the concert I told Zohar about how I might have missed the whole thing. He asked me: 'what do you think would have happened if you had smoked that pipe and arrived late?' I felt a particular kind of squinting forming in my eyes. The same kind that I observed in my dog. I was ready to terminate his furry soul for suggesting such a thing. He took my hand and said: 'relax.'

Zohar wrote a piece for this lot of childless witches called *Echad*, or *One*, and I understood what he meant by pulsating at unison with another's heart: $D - - T - - T -$. So we also drummed for one another. Each in our own way. The collective beat of twenty-two joined the flow. Zohar's gaze following our fingers reminded us to think the connection: 'As above, so below.' And yet, while his drum electrified vertically, his gaze established a horizontal line as well. We were all under him, but only because he insisted on no hierarchy. 'I'm here to serve' is his mantra, and one hears it as the *doum* on

34

the drum, the very vehicle that creates dynamics. Zohar left us all flat on our bellies, supplicating, or flat on our backs, ecstatically contemplating the stars.

People there asked me whether I drum for shamanic purpose. While I replied in the negative, I told them about various archaic techniques of trance-inducing rituals, paraphrasing Mircea Eliade.[5] By drumming, most shamans of the world believe that they can fly to the Cosmic Tree. The skin of the drum is revived through a pulsing touch and the voice. The sounds taken together recall various spirits. As such, the drum is used as a means for ascension. The shaman is a medium who creates a correspondence between theriomorphic ancestors, the mythical subterranean beings nurturing the roots of the tree, and the cosmic branches holding the dead souls.

The way Zohar slid his fingers on the drum, pressing on it as if to demonstrate my point, created a swishing sound that always made me bite my lips. His moist hand tapping gently on the dead skin reanimated some other worlds which I was trying to mix in with my own. 'So, you are an alchemist,' a biochemist interested in drumming asked at our last supper. 'I don't know about me,' I said, 'but I know that Zohar is one. He has the right ingredients, and he knows how to mix them. He puts into his playing neither too much, nor too little, but exactly as much as it's necessary. He takes balance and control to sublime levels. The level where we can all hope.'

A few German percussionists insisted that I was a *kräuter-hexe*, a healing herbalist witch with a penchant for synthesizing philosophies and religions. 'Drumming is a form of divination,' I said to them. 'The drummer summons the sun and the moon, the underworld, the Lord of the Dead, *and...* the *Echad.*' 'You will hear spoken in symbols, what you already know,' I told another, who called me 'a healing Tarotist.' 'The shamans of the tundra Yurak call their drum a singing bow,' I further said, 'and they offer horse-meat to the master of the drum.'

In hindsight, I'm now thinking that I did an awful lot of preaching on this trip. But what could we offer Zohar? Perhaps an acknowledgment of what we are, including the ghost notes. I recall saying this to the ones calling me names: 'I'm all these things because of the magic of noise and the magic of music. We're all summoned by him already, by his sensual splendor.'

Then suddenly I realized that Ross Daly's stray dogs that he likes to rescue, some five of them, were in the middle of our jamming circle. No one summoned them, except for the drums and the promise of my hand on their belly.

'You have to pull the light to yourself,' another Kabbalist drummer said, and then concluded that I was 'a funny woman.' I don't know about the funny part, but fun I had. In Zohar's company one thought of him as a pulsating light. Splendor *is* embedded in his name. I said to him: 'If Zohar is a *zoharic* pulse, then drumming must return to you. We're all childless witches waiting for the arrival of the first beat. Trembling.'

1   See Susan Greenwood's works, all published by Berg, Oxford: *Magic, Witchcraft, and the Otherworld*, 2000; *The Nature of Magic: An Anthropology of Consciousness*, 2005; *The Anthropology of Magic*, 2009.

2   See *The Poetic Edda*. Lokasenna, verse 26 and Snorri Sturluson's *Ynglinga Saga 3*. In Heimskringla: eða Sögur Noregs Konunga.

3   See Gershom G. Scholem's *Major Trends in Jewish Mysticism* (Jerusalem: Schocken 1941, 3d revised ed: reprint 1961), p. 229.

4   See Nicolaj de Mattos Frisvold's study, *Pomba Gira and the Quimbanda of Mbùmba Nzila* (Scarlet Imprint, 2011).

5   See especially Mircea Eliade's seminal book, *Shamanism: Archaic Techniques of Ecstasy* (Princeton University Press, 1964).

Dance

¶I'M SQUINTING. I'm watching a domestic drama. Japanese Butoh dancers Carlotta Ikeda and Ko Murobushi are having a quarrel on stage. *Aï-Amour*. She wants him. He wants her not. He regrets it though. That's why he brings her flowers. She takes them and smashes them to the ground. Why? There's more to this than I can tell. I want to tell. But how? I imagine starting with this question addressed to the man: Why bring her flowers if you don't want to be with her? Why this form of politeness? The ship is sinking. Literally.

We're here with drama, TV drama. The setting is a ship and two lovers on their last breath. They fight. No, she fights. She slaps him. Repeatedly. He receives her hand in humility. If only the earth could open up to eat him; eat his shame. But they're floating on water. They go with the flow, as they say, literally. Only the soul is in pieces, responding to the staccato of the slapping hands. And heads. And yet. They are one soul, rhyming with the water their ship sails on. We don't see any water to begin with. Only the device that keeps the ship tight, a steel door with two turning wheels that lock the ship, preventing the water from coming in.

The lovers are not on the top deck. They are at the bottom. What is this room called? I doubt it's called 'the womb,' though it looks like the womb. I had to look up the name to be precise, read on naval architecture. Yes, the bottom of the ship is called 'the hull.' Wind blows against the hull, and waves run into it. I was surprised to learn about metal fatigue. Engineers make a lot of fuss about it, about iron and steel having a fatigue limit. How appropriate in the context of dancing, when pressure is applied to the body, exhausting it.

So our lovers are locked up in a hermetically tight room. Light is reflected in the reddish walls of iron, making us think of what we imagine life is like on Mars. These two butoh dancers are not just lovers. They are martial artists. Or, *are* they lovers? Have they been lovers? I don't know, but I have a hunch. As I'm not into the literature of gossip, I'll refrain from making statements other than the creative type, the type that invites to a certain mood of romanticizing a vision.

I never saw this performance live, first happening in Stockholm in 1993, just a rendition of it as part of the documentary *Aï-Amour: Carlotta Ikeda and her Butoh* (2001). Kamal Musale directs. In addition to the original dance choreographed by Carlotta Ikeda and Ko Murobushi, we have another dance called cinematography, the dance of light with angles and constrained shots. The camera zooms in and out of the dancers in their setting, shifting the perspective too, messing with our sense of the vertical. Things are not flat here, though we find the lovers often horizontal, rolling on the floor full of sand. When they stand, their heads meet head on. The *tête-à-tête* encounter is literal.

I'll offer here an analysis of this 10-minute performance by way of describing what's happening, because I find what's happening fascinating in terms of the point about childlessness that I want to make.

Let's start with the tension between vertical and horizontal representations. If we think of the general metaphors we live by, we note the following: people and things standing tall are privileged over the people and things that lie flat. Culturally speaking you have as yet to hear someone talking about aiming for the flat point. No. Everybody aims for the high, the tall, the phallic expression. Power is thought of as having a vertical direction. *Aï-Amour* also operates with this idea. Up until a point. On the one hand, there's a clear message that power is lost when one lays flat. On the other hand, the vulnerable is palpable in this performance. This is pleasing to the ones invested in reverting the conservative hierarchy by assigning power to the horizontal. Currently there's no end to the virtues tied to being a victim, down, depressed, in agony or pain. All of this 'horizontal' state is now marked as a source of immense creative potential. I don't know about this, especially since I'm generally suspicious of the strategies of replacing one dominant system with another, whose aim is to become equally dominant. I'm interested in other manifestations of the vulnerable than the ones in which the vulnerable is merely a vehicle for more capitalist commodification.

I'm not at all convinced by the current discourse about tactics of empowering victims by upraising their vulnerable stories. I hear the martial artists laughing. Yielding power is not the same as self-indulgence. Not even when one is in love. Power is power. There's no such thing as power in the high or power in the low. One is not more powerful because of the odd, strange, or painful experience, better known as a story. One is not more powerful because one is good at making decisions and staying on track, also better known as a story. Just as power is power, so with stories. A story is a story. There are good stories and bad stories, but at the level of form, a story is a story. It has a beginning, a middle, and an end. Even postmodern stories that resist such reductionism and trivialization follow this formula, one way or another.

The story of *Aï-Amour* lasts exactly 10 minutes. But it's enough for an efficient story to emerge. We're here with quite a conventional story. A lost lover comes back to the woman he loves. A classic. It's not sure why, but that's what makes it interesting. However, what makes this performance more than just interesting is the fact that the woman seems to know why the man comes back to her. Let's see. In lock down in the hull, suffering from fatigue already, the two dancers interrogate the possibility to love, or rather, to still love beyond the realm of feeling and emotion. Whoa, is that possible? That's the question.

Now, what is not so immediately apparent is the fact that this is a performance that has form in focus, rather than content that manipulates with our preconceived notions of what love is and how it's supposedly informed by feeling. What gives it away though is the appearance of a turtle right at the beginning of the performance, suggesting that if we are to get it, the drama, it will be the slow way. The turtle's function as a cameo for the Japanese *kame*, a turtle, is reminiscent of the function of a Greek chorus in a tragedy, voicing collectively a comment on the dramatic action. The turtle here is alone and silent, but in its solitary, quiet presence, it articulates a forceful, yet subtle message. In slang, *kame* in Japanese means both a penis, as the turtle's neck resembles the male organ, and possibly a cuckold. So, here comes the penis to do what? The woman acts forcefully towards the man, grabbing him by his head, slapping it and kissing it too, as if this head was not attached to anything. We could say that this is a dance about heads and what they can do independently of the rest of their sensual and emotional body. I find this fascinating.

The beginning of the performance starts with these words on screen from the director: 'After 10 years of separation Carlotta Ikeda reunites with her partner Ko Murobushi, and creates with him the dance *Aï-Amour.*'[1] Splendid. What happened in the meantime? Work partners? Love partners? Ikeda left Japan in the early 80s and settled in France. According to her own admission she got tired of the patriarchal approach to dance. She got tired of men running the show from a self-proclaimed position of superiority. Murobushi joined her and together they started the all-women dance company Ariadone. They choreographed for Ariadne's thread. We are still slow in getting this one. It worked to great acclaim.

44

Now the two dancers meet again to go through a new passage, or is it an old story they're rehearsing? *Aï-amour,* indeed. For a short while Murobushi was married to the mysterious and delicate butoh dancer Urara Kusanagi.[2] It didn't work out. *Aï-Amour.* We can only speculate here, for who has access to the inner life of geniuses? Regardless of the personal story, as a co-creator with Ko, Carlotta is full of force. No fragility here. If she gets on the floor, it's because she wants to catch the man by surprise, size him up from an angle that's this close to the command: 'now, attack him now. His guard is down. He is slow in perceiving...'

I'm telling this story backwards, but that's because the dance starts with the back. His back at her back. But we only see his back to begin with. Contracting. Expanding. Then the camera is on her. She is calm at first, and we almost perceive a smile, as if saying 'finally this turtle, *kame,* has come.' From his behind, she then takes hold of him in a tight embrace. It only lasts a few seconds. The focus is on her hands in possessive mode. But then she throws him off her in a rotation. This rejection has the form of a question: 'why?' he is wondering, and I also want to know. Why? Why what? No matter. Just the 'why' is enough. 'Why' has a centrifugal force in it. In fact it's so strong that before we know it, both dancers are on the floor. Rolling. She, a crouching tiger. He, a panther. Or wait. He's not happy with that. One of his eyes nullifies the possibility of the agile master. It squints right after an impressive jump. Now what? If not the panther then which one? The animal body is in focus. How about a turtle? Let's settle on the turtle. We don't see the turtle yet, but it's here already in his gaze. Then the meeting of heads. After rolling on the floor at high speed, their heads meet up. They are head to head in an extreme close-up. Then the tension stops. It's a Zen moment.

We want to ask impatiently, can they rise, the lovers, when they're on the floor like this, attracting and repelling one another? But rise to what? I wonder if other dance critics posed this question. I haven't seen a proper analysis. There's duality here, contraction and expansion. Ten minutes of this law of the universe is filled with an intense dance about precisely that, contraction and expansion. That's the form. But there's also something else here. The cameraman is on to it, this something else. He shoots the lovers from strange angles. The gazes are both elongated and short. What unites them is the squinting. Carlotta is squinting a lot in this one, exhibiting a tight nerve. Every time she squints, I also squint. That's the form. But what we both squint at is the heart, the heart of no heart.

In *The Heart Sutra* we read: 'There is no form. No eyes, no ears, no mouth.' I'm following Carlotta's eyes on Ko. They are beyond form, beyond the mouth, letting out a sigh, *aï-amour!* Ay, this love that hurts... *Ai-Amour* is a play on the Japanese kanji letters *ai*, for love, and the French idea of possession, *ai, avoir.* Can there be love without possessing? Although you'd think this is a question of content, it's actually a question of form. We want to know, because when it comes down to it, it's *all* about form. Love is about form. Marriage is about form. The notion of children is about form. You'd think that all these concepts enacted as major life events are about the meaning of life, about life's very significant content. But it's not. It's about form. And yet there is no form. *The Heart Sutra* says so, and the physicists say so.

Form must follow a vision. Many confuse having children with having a vision. No one thinks in logical terms. False correlations abound. Everyone wants emotions and to get soft in their knees. 'I do' is still a powerful speech act said in church or some other consecrated venue. It melts the heart. The idea of your children holding your hand when you die is also pretty powerful. Never mind the actual reality of this fantasy. But since when does reality beat fiction? Some insist all this is real... enough. Fair enough. But even as such, we're still with just a form of something that we have as yet to actually grasp. What is all this kneeling all about, asking her to marry you? Ironically what melts the heart is precisely the opposite of clarity. What do we find there? Constructed meaning. The opposite of the obvious is the idea that *all* of this has meaning. But what meaning? Ikeda and Murobushi had no children. Somehow they managed to escape the meaning of life and go all in on form.

Let's rewind. Imagine this film, *Aï-Amour,* that I can only reproduce in words. You can watch it if you like, but watching it is not a prerequisite for getting the point. I'm telling a story here, and as you've heard already, a story is a story. Don't take

47

my insistence on this as an act of arrogant patronizing. It's not. What I'm pointing to is the magnificence of the obvious. So, in this film we have two heads banging on one another. She initiates the banging. We don't know who came on the ship first, or who initiated the idea of the reunion.

But she initiates the play of gazes. Although hermetically closed in the hull, there's weather outside. We can hear the wind. We hear thunder and rain in the background. This is famed filmmaker Kurosawa's chief trick. 'There has to be rain in it, for motion to flow naturally,' he said, and he was right. Although we don't see any rain, the enchantment works. If it rains on Mars or on a sinking boat, then maybe something gets saved.

After the first embrace and the rolling on the floor in the sand, the dancers' heads meet. Their foreheads gyrate at the meeting point. Then she grabs him by the collar of his shirt. Violently. She lifts him up with a lot of force, then puts him down. Also with a lot of force. She grabs his head again, slaps his cheeks, and then brings the head close to her forehead so she can bang on it with her own head. Then a kiss. He receives her kiss on top of his head without a motion or a word. All of this happens on the vertical axis. Then they're both down. She, like a reptile. He, on his knees. Hand to forehead. What do we read in this cliché? Regret? Let's go with regret because of what happens next.

She approaches him, slithering like a snake. He, a monkey. They gyrate, chasing each other's tails, casting a magic circle in the sand. Their heads meet again. We reach a deflating point, with both dancers breathing out in fetus position. Enter the turtle. Now the man is flat on his back, pulling away from the woman. She grabs his legs. There's enormous tenderness in her gesture. This is *the* vulnerable moment. He pulls away more resolutely. Her eyes go blank, and she lets go of him. What we read in her eyes is this: 'nothing has changed.' Next, after a few attempts to stand on his own, the man goes down on his knees, leaning heavily on his back, his eyes turned to the ceiling in a moment of rapture, but also one that's open to receiving punishment. He doesn't have to wait too long.

The woman has a large bouquet of red roses in her hands. She starts banging his head with them. We don't see this right away. But we see his forehead bleeding. The next minute, a solitary frenzy. The roses hit the floor and get smashed to pieces. The woman beats the flowers to a pulp, until they disintegrate. A lost red thread.

There's a lot of force in this beating. Ikeda's body displays the kind of power here that I was just talking about, the power that's power, raw power, that is, and as such highly magical.

If this was the 19th century, it would have been argued that such a display of frenzy might have been provoked by the inability to accept the fact that you can't marry your lover and that you can't have his children. Therefore you can't ultimately call yourself respectable. And because you can't call yourself respectable, the only other label available to you is the hysterical. If you can't be the Madonna, you'll the whore. There's no state in between.

Or is there? – apart from the fantasy in the biblical story that references the Apocalyptic figure of Babylon who rides the beast of hell, a figure now appropriated by occultists as *the* redeeming Other, the interstitial woman, the only one capable of saving the world from self-implosion. As this story begs another discussion, I won't get into it here especially since I'm not convinced, but suffice it to say that in the context of the regular domestic drama that's not transgressive, we don't talk about what is not culturally endorsed already. I'm not interested in transgression. I'm interested in the ordinary expression of how we get to the stage of loving without love, and the stage of staying childless without having to explain.

What is the vehicle for getting there? This is where I find *Aï-Amour* interesting. At some point towards the end of the performance both dancers are on a tightrope. One horizontal, he, and one vertical, she. Walking on the tightrope, or rather, as we have it represented here, lying flat on a tightrope or climbing it seems appropriate. Ko Murobushi's body lies flat on the wire, barely holding its balance. Again we're with the notion of some sacrifice of sorts, a form of strange supplication, surrendering to something. What this something is remains undisclosed, unless we want to talk about the loss of power connected to the idea of both wanting it and not wanting it, the woman, that is, or the marriage and children.

In a similar fashion, though going on the vertical plane, the woman is also engaged on the tightrope, trying to climb it. A strange idea, as trying to climb a wire is not only impossible but also futile. In contrast to the man's motion, banging his back against the wire that cuts right through the middle of his body, the woman's body doesn't display despair. Rather, her gaze shows readiness geared towards not caring anymore, her hands gently caressing the wire. She has the common sense, or no sense at all by this time, to realize that since this ship is sinking, it renders all heroic acts of vulnerability redundant. This scene is significant for what it transmits via the wire. The two lovers are not wired, though they *know* the wire and use it, each to their ends. They are both vulnerable in their pain but they are not possessed by their vulnerability. Free from emotions, they are free from desire. Free from desire, they are free from illusion. Bang. The heads are empty of projections.

The final scene features an explosion. The ship is submersed. Both are now in an embrace, as if twins in a womb. They are back to the primordial womb, assuming the position of the fetus again, a butoh obsession *par excellence*, suggestive of how we might recall our first movements. Light does it. Light matters more than emotion, the performance seems to indicate, and we get to see how the light on the stage shifts from the initial belligerent and martial atmospheric force to a soft, white kind of floating in the end, embracing the two that are now entangled in a bubble.

The film ends with the sound of a cuckoo having the last word in it. This irony is not lost on the viewer who remembers the dance mimicking the movements of animals. But it was the turtle that opened the drama and the cuckoo that ended it. There's no other form to life than what we can say about our 'enter and exit' experiences.

Aï-Amour is a perfect enchantment that deconstructs our expectations of what we think the bodies are made to perform by virtue of a presupposed naturalness of being. We come into the world, we live, and we die. That's the form. That's the formula for our stories. Anything else in between is paying lip service to expectations. We may tend to one another, especially when in love, but this tending to one another does not equal being on the same page. Domestic drama always follows the cuckoo. Someone is always as slow as a turtle in the relationship to grasp just what the other needs or wants. Thus we are never on the same page unless we go beyond the cliché of marital union, motherhood, parenting, and civic responsibility. But who *can* go beyond? Most don't ask themselves: Who do we marry for? Who do we have children for?

Who do we call ours? Grasping at concepts, or what we like to call, 'the big mysteries of life' made up of our own lumping together notions of love, childrearing, parenting, and civic responsibility is the fastest and safest route towards forgetfulness. We forget to dance. We are adept at dancing to societal tunes, cultural trends, and symbolic representations of power. But the question still remains. If we acknowledge the idea that all of this is just form and a formality, then who do we have children for? I imagine Carlotta Ikeda answering: 'not for myself, and not for anyone else.' She did say this though: 'There is a desire that vibrates inside me, and for many years I have been in search of that precise point where the trembling lies… It is perhaps this wave of vibration that is the source of my dancing.'[3] Let us heed attention to the bewitching power that enabled her to say that, to perform as Medea towards her end, so we can move more swiftly through our stories.

I dance with stones. I give them the names of dead people and together we perform a memory act. Not long ago, as I was walking on the beach I found a pebble, well, a hag stone, to be more precise. I decided it was Michael Riffaterre as a Romantic hero. As I looked through the stone's hole I got transported to Riffaterre's office at Columbia University in New York, the French department. Twenty years earlier. On my 'visiting scholar' exchange visit, he was my supervisor on my first doctoral dissertation on the notion of the fragment in literature. I presented Riffaterre with some pretentious ideas. He said, 'fuck philosophy, I wish all metaphysicians would hang,' making a gesture that followed his eyes, concretely going upwards and upstairs, where the philosophy department was. 'Give me something concrete,' he said to me. 'Concrete like what?' I asked him. 'Like cemeteries and the moonlight,' he said. Immediately I felt butoh dancer Tatsumi Hijikata's famous golden phallus shooting right through me. Riffaterre and I did a butoh dance of darkness right then and there in his office in broad daylight, in the form of literary legs and metaphysical poetry without metaphysics in it.

And no, in case you're wondering. We didn't have sex à la the stereotypical expectation: man in power bangs infatuated student. It was more interesting than that. Because it was a dance. One that started in 1999. I met Riffaterre at Aalborg University, where he was on a lecture tour. After his final talk he looked for me in the lecture hall in the break before the Q&A session. He came up to me and without any introduction asked me if I wanted to go to New York. I said yes before he explained. The only thing he said, following such bluntness, was that it had been years since he had experienced a burning gaze from someone sitting in the last row in a room where three hundred other people were also sitting.

I'm not sure how much Riffaterre knew about butoh dancers, but he had a good sense of arriving. He was a poetry specialist with a keen eye on tension. He wasn't interested in the tension *in your face*. He preferred the imperceptible kind, as that was the kind that held truth in its fiction.[4]

The founder and inventor of the modern dance butoh, Tatsumi Hijikata, played with this kind of tension too. How do you arrive for something special? Through feeling it? You'd think that feeling is the usual suspect. Think again. What we call feeling is not an innocent thing, mysterious and full of mystical power. Feeling is subject to language. You feel exactly that which you can conjure into language. Nothing more, nothing less. Poets and dancers of caliber know this. The others who don't know this wade in their own feelings, imitating. They call this wading 'originality,' because feeling is subjective, they claim. But the reality is that they are incapable of original improvisation which requires the calibration of tension that's imperceptible.

Hijikata's most famous dance is called *The Rebellion of the Body*. He performed it in Japan in 1958. In it he has a sequence where he dons a strapped on golden phallus that he uses to bang on a mirror, a steel wall. He was frantic in his express effort to penetrate the hard surface. Such futility... That was the point, to bang on the futile so people having lost their sense of distinction might get it. Critics called this act an act of resistance, an act of rejecting Western values that had started to take over the so-called Japanese soul. But what everyone is in agreement about is the *in your face* act. Beyond the jumping around naked, flashing an emaciated body attached to *the* object of desire, a golden and erect phallus, Hijikata sports an imperceptible tension. It's the tension that makes him arrive in your soul, the tension that makes you perform a dance in which you let an idea kiss the ghosts you conjure.

I get this notion when I see Hijikata's 'heir,' Ko Murobushi, dance to music by ABBA, the tuned called *Arrival*, though in an arrangement by Mike Oldfield where the tempo is heightened. As such, it hits the hips of the dancer in a swaying that releases the tension, while gathering it in the hands, lost in a pettiskirt that's almost pink. What imitation are we here with now? When Riffaterre asked me to present him with something concrete, what he wanted was for me to stop imitating a certain embodiment of the academic, the scholar. He didn't conjure the moon either because he wanted more feeling from me – he was smarter than that. Rather, what he wanted was to test my self-reliant spine. He decided I was fearless, but how strong was my spine? In my butoh dance in his office I took it upon myself to hang all metaphysicians. Did I do it because that's what he wanted? No, because that would have been giving in to some field of emotion devoid of individual thought. Without this thought, there's no true emotion.

There's emotion and feeling that we all experience, as do the animals. Hijikata was brilliant in portraying chickens. Some marveled at his imitating power. But that's because they weren't looking closely. What Hijikata did was far more advanced than merely imitating. Because he was also a childless witch who understood the emotions and feelings of animals, he was good at posing true questions. The ones who picked up on this particular legacy learned how to view their bodies in the moment of impersonation. They all performed without performing. A restless chicken? No problem. As a tool, what is its function? Ikeda and Murobushi asked this question of their bodies as a tool. What can the body do when a turtle or a cuckoo? A hen gets very upset if you won't let her hatch her eggs. A dog will love you forever if you're kind to it. But that's not advanced. To succumb to suffering or the promise of bliss is not advanced. What's advanced is to ask this question when feeling arises: what's it to it?

As for the body, Hijikata demonstrated that it's more than a modern holy cow holding primacy over what we can see is the case with utmost clarity. We feel good when we move. Can we leave it at that? For some bizarre reason, most butoh dancers that came after Hijikata decided that the sensual body is our everything and all. This is all fine, but when the 'everything and all' excludes the part that's called language that's constitutive of the very idea of the body, then the 'everything and all' is lacking in both form and content.

For Carlotta Ikeda the body is a tool. This is a whole other perspective on the body, especially the woman's body, forever subject to patriarchal sanctions, regulations and restrictions. When Ikeda furthermore says that her body is a *phenomenal* tool,[5] one that she took years to learn, we detect a humble demeanor towards recognizing that the phenomenal is both of the nature of appearance and the marvelous, in other words fictional and hence unreal. Feeling put in the service of the body as a utility tool is not a popular idea, as such a notion is entirely devoid of the fantasy of crossing thresholds to some presupposed realm of utmost creativity. But the creative resides in how you *think* about it, not how you feel about it, when feeling is nothing but part of a particular grammar and vocabulary, subject to the games of the intricate mind.

In extrapolation, just think about how easy the world of a woman would be if she thought of her body as a tool put in the service of a number of things. You may put your body in the service of having children, but then you may as well put it in the service of something else. Put it this way, suddenly the children idea as part of the meaning of life appears ridiculous. What I'm interested in is the point when there are no emotional attachments in the attitude and conceptual thinking about the body, when the body is not privileged without just cause. The notion that the body is a sacred temple becomes completely erroneous when we try a humble dethroning of it.

Indeed, when we think of it in these terms, we realize what is at stake in the idea of a performance that's more than the sum of what and who we can imitate. Few are actually capable of such a performance, with some coming close via insightful improvisation. Going back to Tracy Emin's statements about the consequences of being childless, one might be tempted to say that being childless is an art in and of itself, with those performing it resembling gods descended from heaven. But when art transgresses the conventional commodification of set ideas, it gets sent to hell. Just think: you can't pass judgment on people's decisions to get emotional about the grand events in life, such as, falling in love, getting married, getting the children and a house, a dog, and a meaningful job that ensures the wellbeing of the next generation.

Society and culture will tell us that such things are in alignment. True, if we talk about metaphysicians in the dark performing for an audience that's not even interested. On the other hand, there's nothing wrong with cultural ideals, except for the fact that they are empty of substance. As for the form of the domestic story, I'd say it has little value from an aesthetic point of view. It has little value because its premise is based on a false notion of stability. For instance, no one wants to mention risk, the unpredictable, or the randomness that can befall the general state of happiness of most households. If anyone were to mention the possibility of divorce right at the moment when the utterance 'I do' occurs, it would be deemed inappropriate. It would kill everyone's pleasure felt at knee level. But wouldn't such a remark fall in the category of stating the obvious probability for a split, as high as the other thing that's called the promise to hold it together 'until death do us part?'

The whole circus about the value of feeling is due to the fact that people have lost their ability to tell a performance from the real thing. This is easiest to see in dance, which is why I refer to it here. It is my contention that a woman's experience of being childless comes close to the aim in butoh to get beyond performance. When Hijikata disseminated his ideas about non-performing through strict choreography, he combined irreconcilable antagonisms.[6] 'Here's how *not* to imitate. Here's how *not* to improvise.' Right. What else is left? Butoh dancers *almost* took this question to their heart. I say 'almost' because in my own assessment as a critical studies and art analyst, what I've realized after having watched countless butoh dancers is that most of them cannot *not* perform.

While butoh as a dance form has conquered the world with its invitation to the exploration of inner landscapes, not all who have embraced butoh have understood what 'inner landscape' is all about, many confusing the concept with accessing self-help, using symbolic imagery as a tool. But is that it? How can butoh, the dance of utter darkness — Hijikata's coinage for it — be about symbolic expression? And of what? Darkness itself? The womb? A childless woman's womb?

Not even Ikeda could quite wrap her head around what defines the 'inner landscape' or what personal geographical boundaries it might have, apart from saying that it's a place to be shared as one shares a dream. In her own refutation of butoh as an expression of something sacred, she said the following: 'It is nothing more than a custom impregnating everyday life. The essential thing for me is to convey an emotion, to get in touch with the audience and make them dream. And I am sorry if they miss the symbols.'[7] Why is this childless witch wavering, apologizing for not succeeding in making the symbols obvious? In this, I see her departing from Hijikata's radical idea, hitting a stonewall made up of the sudden conviction that conveying an emotion is what butoh is about.

In its current popularity, butoh is seen as being about shamanic expressions of accessing higher levels of consciousness, with dancers claiming that the sensual body alone, independent of its cognitive faculty, has the capacity to cross thresholds, thus placing the dancer in a position beyond language, or a place where memory functions as an *ur* experience of the state in the womb, prior to birth. On this, I like the work of Alkistis Dimech,[8] butoh dancer and childless occultist invested in the rise of feminine power via witchcraft currents, but I'm not convinced by the argument that the body precedes desire. Isn't desire constituted by language the same way the body is? Any performance of a goddess avatar through dance is exactly that, a performance, not the essence of the obvious that conveys more than an emotion that others can dream of.

What I myself am looking for is more than the representation of the emaciated body, or the body that goes through ordeals in order to gain access to secret mysteries, high and low. In terms of practice, one may even ask, what's so special about the performance of fasting? Nothing. Everybody can do it, even the ones who are lousy at discipline. Thus my point is that while there are states of knowledge that are not linguistically contingent, relaying this knowledge is impossible, as you need words for it, framing devices. Performances. So my point, again, is that if we are to ask true questions of just what form the performances we participate in have, then we must consider our motivations when we insist on feelings being something other than plain performance.

Sometimes I perform the dance of utter darkness under the gaze of the human skulls in my private Zendo. I conjure the childless witches, and together we go beyond all lamentation.

1 The performance of *Aï-Amour* from 1993 was first released in 2001 as part of a documentary, *Aï-Amour: Carlotta Ikeda and her Butoh*. The film directed by Kamal Musale features the work of dancer and choreographer Carlotta Ikeda and her collaboration with dancer and choreographer Ko Murobushi.

2 See the *Ko Murobushi Archives* [https://ko-murobushi.com/eng/ Last accessed on December 1, 2020]

3 See Laurencine Lot's book, *Carlotta Ikeda - La danse Buto et au-delà*, that combines photographs from iconic performances with Ikeda's statements about butoh (Favre, 2005).

4 See *Fictional Truth*, a small book by Michael Riffaterre that makes big points about our perceptions (The Johns Hopkins University Press, 1990).

5 See an excerpt from an interview with Marcelle Michelle for Le Monde, 1984, in *Carlotta Ikeda - La danse Buto et au-delà* by Laurencine Lot, p. 170 (Favre, 2005).

6 See for instance the introduction 'Hijikata Tatsumi: The Words of Butoh' by Kurihara Nanako in TDR (1988-) Vol. 44, No. 1 (Spring, 2000), p. 10-28. The MIT Press.

7 See an excerpt from an interview with Marcelle Michelle for *Le Monde*, 1984, in *Carlotta Ikeda - La danse Buto et au-delà* by Laurencine Lot, p. 169 (Favre, 2005).

8 See *The Brazen Vessel* by Alkistis Dimech and Peter Grey (Scarlet Imprint 2019).

Voice

INDEED, BEFORE HER CHILDREN, Medea was a fine witch. After her children, the more miserable she became, the more powerful also, though as 'the bad' had already incurred, the price of power was life itself in its manifestation of loss. Between Euripides' depiction in the Greek antiquity of the character of the powerful witch Medea[1] and the modern, contemporary filmatization of the tragedy by Pier Paolo Pasolini (1969) featuring the glorious, yet here mute opera singer Maria Callas[2], not much has changed. We record only imperceptible shifts in the emphasis on the dance of seduction, the trembling in desire and death, the thundering no – 'No, you cannot have the bodies of your murdered children, your children murdered by me' – and grace, for is there the thing – love, or revenge – that has any purpose?

What makes mythical characters endure the passing of time is the fact that they are always already composites of all that we desire, fear, and oppose. These three elements make a classic. Throw into the cauldron of creativity an iconic image and you're set.

Pier Paolo Pasolini's filmatization of *Medea* is heavily invested in character, above all in the character that Maria Callas delivered. Up until his death when he himself was murdered, Pasolini produced some of the best films ever by insisting on using common people on the film sets rather than professional actors. In fact it took him a few grand masterpieces before he actually hired professionals. The Callas intervention, as I like to call it, is different. Maria Callas was a revered icon of her generation, an opera singer of the highest caliber throughout the 1950s, yet with a love life to cry about. The only child she might have had was presumably aborted in 1966, due to the social inconvenience called, 'when the lover, Aristotle Onassis, is wooing the Other Woman, Jackie Kennedy, the widow of the murdered president JFK,[3] you stand back.'

Callas had a tragic love life, taken straight out of a tragic Greek drama, but Pasolini wasn't interested in her personal grief, or operatic voice as *voiced*. He was interested in her grief and operatic voice as *image*. The way he positioned her voice as image, via the oracular in poetic language, is by combining violence and excitement in a bundle of awareness about human nature, suggesting, namely, that we never are what we think we are. For the entire duration, iconic opera singer Callas barely utters any words. And that's not because she sings them instead. What's going on? Why use a voice icon in a

66

film, and then have her pretty mute? Medea was a bad witch, the old story tells us, suggesting that powerful women don't speak a lot because they don't need to. They just do things, bad things. If we look at the archaic connotation of the Latin/ Italian verb *facere*, we note that the word implies creating a spell. Contemporary Romania has retained this, and you can still go to a gypsy and ask for a *facatura*, a spell, or a magical working whose aim is often to make another drop dead.

Pasolini gets at this very notion. Powerful women are beyond language. Medea only speaks when she has something to say. And when she says it, it manifests as a spell. Her desires are formulated as spells, and so are her fears. There is a point in the film when Medea fears that she lost contact with her old gods, but through dream incubation and meditation, she returns to a renewed form of empowerment. The connection may have been lost, but not so the technique of recalling the old powers.

Let's rewind: Medea, the very bad witch of olden times predating any form of modernity, steals the Golden Fleece from her people who are in contact with all that is holy in nature, and therefore also completely unnatural, at least according to Pasolini's seductive genius. 'How can nature be natural', he asks using the voice and body of the centaur in the film, a voice that waxes philosophical not only on the nature of everything, but also on the nature of inquiry itself. 'How can nature be natural when in every twisted sky or tree there's a god?' That's actually a very good question. Pagan

Pasolini doesn't merely direct a film, but makes sure to sit on just about every threshold, every turning point in the story, in order to make sure that every thought is heard and recorded. Not voice. Thought. Here, particularly the thought of going from a state of natural witchcraft – embodied by nature's ability to enchant itself as recognized by people – to culture, the point when awareness of the magical nature of nature is lost.

The first turning point in the film is when Medea is portrayed as a high priestess not to be messed with, or in lay terms, a bad witch on the path of childlessness. She is skillful in her craft of being one with nature. And yet, it is exactly at the point of recognizing this skill, that is, the skill to navigate nature in flow, that the question about the value of naturalness to be above any process of cultivation arises. What is there to cultivate is not the conquest of nature, but the ability to recognize your place in it. So now the bad witch Medea is the good witch, as she is grounded and well versed in communing with the 'unnaturalness' of the gods.

The turning point comes when the childless witch decides that she wants to be a woman who elopes with her lover in order to become a housewife and do the rest, have children. She remembers her skills though, when there's no reason for her any longer to serve her unfaithful husband. As the play and the film depict Medea's return to her truth, walking back to the poison path, there's the first clear indication of how, by way of culture, there's no free lunch. You don't go from motherhood to your childless state without paying for it. Pasolini, a stern anti-capitalist makes a strong statement here, by putting the price of all cultural transactions in your face. As far as culture is concerned, you can't make a move without paying for it. As far as nature is concerned, you move by way of flowing with it, above any symbolic capital. The transaction coin here is simply called 'the obvious.'

But who likes the obvious, the simple? 'What if the simple is too simple,' the insidious in culture asks, with the feeble-minded already all over the concept, participating in the invention of one more complicated idea after the other. If there's anything that lacks obviousness is the notion that, while it's always fine for the husband to repudiate the wife, it is not so where the woman is concerned. The woman can never just say, 'I'm out of here,' and then be merrily on her way. First she has to burn the place down, and in the process hurt herself before anyone takes her seriously. When the eyebrows are also raised, the label gets sticky: 'crazy woman.'

Medea, according to Pasolini, was looking for the logic of this, when she decided that the ways of culture were too complex for her. As the obvious appears to her clearly in her vision of revenge, she sends off fire to burn her husband's new wife as she stands there in her wedding dress, and then poisons the children. The man who only learned the ways of culture, granting him entitlement rights, now also stands there sheepish, lamenting: 'Give me my children's bodies, so I can bury them.' Medea says, 'no.' Nature wins the match, with Medea finding moral justification for her revenge precisely in the obvious. Let's rewind some more: As we witness at the beginning of the film the human sacrifice and thirst for blood to be used ritually on crops, we realize that what drives the narrative forward is the mixture of thrill in seeing another bite the dust, fear, and relief – 'gosh, I'm glad it's not me this time' – and awe of the gods, who are just sexy and cool, or plain hot, to use contemporary pagan self-help vocabulary.

The mortals in the film are not given a lot of agency, but it's clear that they possess desires, fears, and a sense of resigning in the face of escalating conflict. If the weather gods oppose you, you must do what you have to, kill somebody and get on with the program. Meanwhile, the ones who can speak with the fire and don the chain of bones on their lavish costumes orchestrate what we all want: to rise above ordeals, and through sheer passion to allow for visions to envelop us; to get smarter and more commonsensical.

Here is where I think that there's a point of identification with the mythical character, as Medea embodies love and hate, passion and dispassion in equal proportion. When Medea decides to go against the cheating husband, by setting fire to the bridal gown and the bride in it, and then killing off her own children, what gives her the ultimate courage to go through with her calculated acts of strength is justice.

I imagine Pasolini kneeling in front of the tragic Maria Callas, when he shot her from below so that the audience can get a very good view of her stature, power, and embodied invocation. And what does she invoke as the greatest power in her magic? Justice. 'Oh God, Justice so dear to God, Light of the Sun', she goes, and she leaves everyone bedazzled. The curse is then rendered unto the man, poison prepared, and strong visualizations of the future horror rehearsed. Medea is not kidding. She knows her stuff and is unrelenting. She desires her revenge almost as much as she desires to fuck the ingrate one more time. Fuck him she does, with a smile of her lips and a spark of complicity in her eyes. She is, after all, a powerful woman, one who is not ruled by the delusion of feeling.

Thrice in the film we hear characters telling Medea how she's feared by the ordinary mortals. The King of Corinth himself insists on repeating it to her. She is respected for her craft, but this respect stemming from people's fear of her brings her nothing but banishing from the social order. Her ability as a master strategist doesn't exactly put her on any throne, or at least in charge of the military force, even though, lord only knows, she deserves it. Not that she gives a damn. But is it fair? Is it really fair to fear the powerful woman merely because she knows things? Is it fair to repudiate her because she knows the gods, because she knows how to negotiate with them, be a vessel for them?

It seems that what we all desire is justice. What we all have an aversion of is immutable justice. What we all oppose is the law. But what do we really want? Power. How do we want it? Served in bed. And what are we prepared to do if power is denied us? Magic. The myth says, 'murder,' but never mind.

What we must understand is that magic makes the world go round. Pasolini makes this very clear. Medea's magic is what is has always been: the fire within. Civilization tames it. But the barbaric sorceress resists. She loses her power when she becomes aware of how clueless her man is. A sorceress without the other who understands her value is no sorceress. So it's only fair that she starts educating the ignorant.

We see this in the scene where Medea's women in attendance begin to question her motives for choosing sadness — it's ever so sad when the others don't get what you're all about. 'Mistress, you're powerful,' one of the women says feeling pity, 'they say that back in your country you could command fire and air. Why don't you do that anymore?' To this Medea replies that she's not the same woman as then. At the same time she has an epiphany: her eyes go up, her face lights up, and the tension in her muscles disappears. Her body takes charge, ready to receive the voice of magical reason. She realizes that her essence as a sorceress is still the same.

A woman capable of creation is still the same, always already powerful. She feels the magical powers return to her, and through dreams, visions, and omens she understands what she must do, even if her plan is revenge. 'But you can't do this to your lover, Medea,' her servants object, 'you do this to him, you do it to yourself.' To this Medea has only one answer: 'you love me, and you're a woman.' She brings in a subtle form of understanding as the highest expression of experience. Her argument is in the obvious, in the simple

72

declarative statement: 'I am (only) a woman, until you get to watch what I'll do.' That's enough.

As a woman in this sense, she positions herself above the voice of cultural justification and complex reason. What is there to negotiate? Truce? Peace? That would be to recognize conflict as the driving force in life. Is the smoothing of relations a woman's job? Like the rearing of children? The feeding of men and armies? 'Sit quietly, don't disturb your father, he's writing a new essay on women's hysteria,' one can only imagine Freud's wife say to her daughters.

In her avenging mode, Medea is above such petty dualism: peace in the name of the father's comfort. The powerful witch is beyond language. She only speaks, again, when she has something to say. And when she says it, it's a spell. Medea's final 'no' circumscribes her tongue as the door itself, not even slamming compared to the Bible's words:

> And the tongue is a fire: the world of iniquity among our members is the tongue, which defileth the whole body, and setteth on fire the wheel of nature, and is set on fire by hell. But the tongue can no man tame; it is an unruly evil, full of deadly poison (James 3:6-8).

Jason the Argonaut could not tame Medea's oracular tongue. If she silenced herself, it was her own decision. But what was the lesson here? Open your mouth and die? Sing the siren's song and die? Was this the reason why Pasolini chose an opera singer to *not* sing, and hardly speak? What was the purpose of using the voice as image, rather than as a vehicle for sound? What is it that we must not hear, but only see? I like to imagine Medea having gone through all her passions, from learning to loving, yet leave out the children part, say no to bonds, articulate a powerful *non serviam* instead. What would we *hear* from *seeing* such a picture? Her steps, perhaps, of what it must sound like to walk through open doors. Meanwhile, Medea's *no* is heard loud and clear exactly at the moment when she becomes a childless witch, once more.

NO DOOR ON HER MOUTH

Let me make a reference to a passage from Anne Carson's essay 'The Gender of Sound' in her collection of poems and texts *Glass, Irony, and God* (1992).

Madness and witchery as well as bestiality are conditions commonly associated with the use of the female voice in public, in ancient as well as modern contexts. Consider how many female celebrities of classical mythology, literature and cult make themselves objectionable by the way they use their voice. For example there is the heartchilling groan of the Gorgon, whose name is derived from a Sanskrit word **garg* meaning "a guttural animal howl that issues as a great wind from the back of the throat through a hugely distended mouth." There are the Furies whose highpitched and horrendous voices are compared by Aiskhylos to howling dogs or sounds of people being tortured in hell (*Eumenides*). There is the deadly voice of the Sirens and the dangerous ventriloquism of Helen (*Odyssey*) and

74

the incredible babbling of Kassandra (Aiskhylos, *Agamemnon*) and the fearsome hullabaloo of Artemis as she charges through the woods (*Homeric Hymn to Aphrodite*). There is the seductive discourse of Aphrodite which is so concrete an aspect of her power that she can wear it on her belt as a physical object or lend it to other women (*Iliad*). There is the old woman of Eleusinian legend Iambe who shrieks and throws her skirt up over her head to expose her genitalia. There is the haunting garrulity of the nymph Echo (daughter of Iambe in Athenian legend) who is described by Sophokles as "the girl with no door on her mouth" (*Philoktetes*)[4].

Let us think of this image for a while and consider the possibility of a door to mark something other than entering and exiting. Doors mark territories, or rather the separation between them. They can be opened and closed, locked and unlocked, spied upon, or venerated as initiating points. But they also mark the movement of the body from the physical to the metaphysical, from voice to words, from the oracular to the concrete, from science to spirituality.

Body language – literally – is the most physical manifestation of the metaphysical inherent in words. Before words can acquire any meaning they must submit to the symbolic order of assigning power to glyphs: 'if you can name it, it exists,' the Buddhists and the mystic Kabbalists used to say, but they forgot to mention how the body features into all this naming.

In Pasolini's film, most of Medea's talk is done through the gaze. What makes this talk out of the ordinary, aside from Callas's art of the intense expression, is the fact that the gaze is suggestive of a voice's timbre. We often say that the eyes speak the language of desire or the soul, but how is the gaze *heard* exactly? Anne Carson makes a list of the sounds that the mythical women made — most of them childless witches — one more destabilizing than the other, but what of their gazes as voiced powers? In these tales we often hear an instruction directed to the viewer of the 'monsters:' 'don't look at Medusa's head', but what of the gaze that we *hear* in the bones? In most versions of the myth, Helen of Troy was a notorious shapeshifter[5], which implies that she had the ability to change not only her appearance, ironically making men fight for an illusion, but also her voice. We know all about the gazes cast on her by her admirers, but what of the gaze full of trembling timbre that she cast on men?

Just as language — through the timbre of our voice — is the door to our desires, fears, and aversions, so the gaze through the eyes can be expressive of the modulations we find in the voice. Without the body, using the tongue to do its job, there's no naming, there's no madness, witchery, magic, or consecration. Before words can be visualized, the eyes must be trained in their orbs, be vigilant and alert and open to the possibility of love beyond materiality. The same applies to the other emotions. When a witch casts the evil eye on someone, what she does is speak a particular language of the body, often with anger as the drive easily located in the body: sometimes in the fire of the gut, other times in the eye itself, and other times in the knee. Anger as a powerful emotion, like love, can sit just about anywhere in the body. All it requires to locate it is attention via distancing from it, seeing the body as a tool.

Language and desire are indissociable. Saying, 'I want,' is the first step towards the awareness that we have a body that's conscious of fears and desires. The mother projecting love onto her child becomes a form of self-love that the child discovers, a love of being, a love of becoming that which the mother might imagine her child be or become. Culturally speaking, it's necessary to develop a strong ego that ensures a successful navigation through life, often translated as a conflict to be resolved. 'Am I this?' or 'Am I that?' Yet resolving this ambivalence also institutes a crisis, because when we're done deciding, we sense that there's a world beyond identity constructions, beyond the ways of cultural pre-conditioning and societal dictations. That's when we start posing real questions, in a tone of indignation too, suggestive of the fact that we've been spending too much time on nonsense: 'Really, do I actually *have to* be this or that? What if I don't? And who is this *I* anyway? If culture at large refuses to answer this question, culture *&* religion won't, adamantly declaring: 'This *I* is the thing that will go to hell, if you don't obey the rules.'

There is a reason why posing true questions has been banned from most of the civilized worlds: it fucks with you. You just don't want to start the process of self-discovery with 'really?' Welcome to the world of conflict: the world of psycho-pathological expressions of depression, anxiety, attachment, addiction, and compulsion — all labels for what

77

we might as well term 'fictions of the mind.' Welcome also to the world of fixing it. The more suffering subjects, the more helpers – from psychoanalysis as a 'science' to self-help gurus, some cashing in, some pointing out, some asking: 'Really, if you have a problem, *you* have created it.' The underlying structure to all this is a manipulation of language put in the service of the construction of fictions of the self. The medical world itself is not free of fictions either, and one only needs to look at the shifting signifiers that cast depression precisely as a story of the chemistry in the brain, rather than one of psychic disturbance.

To a large extent Pasolini's *Medea* is all about that; about who stands to gain what from providing the golden fleece solutions to life's anguish. So, what's happening? When the project of finding fulfillment in random identifications with 'this' or 'that' fails, mainly because the subject can sense that being enamored in its own identifications with 'this' or 'that' is not 'it,' the subject has the possibility to not only open, but also walk through the door of perception towards the realization of the self *in* relation, that is to say, the self primarily in relation to the language that constitutes it. If there is no 'me against my parents, my lover, the imbecile boss, or the world at large,' then there's nothing to be anxious about. Depression becomes a label, and the anguish of love a kind of self-imposed violence that is exciting and painful at the same time. Imagine what would happen if culture and society started a campaign against comparison: Maiden, Mother,

Crone. It sounds so good. Each of these concepts can fix the self so nicely... Once you can 'relate,' you don't need to ask any more questions. Identity is fixed, settled and cured on all fronts, and you're happy with your lot. You think.

In reality, however, the relational self positions itself at advantage when it allows itself to enter a process of inquiry into the nature of all that befalls it. The process of inquiry into the nature of the self creates the premise for a successful integration of the subject's realization of 'no self.' In Sophocles and Euripides' time, while men were busy chasing the most beautiful construction of Self, *the* woman, Helen, the shapeshifter and ventriloquist, made sure to place herself on a par with Nemesis, whose status as a shapeshifter was much revered because it was rare. And what do all shapeshifting characters have in common? An understanding of the concept of 'no self.' We could argue that the most famous childless witches of the antiquity stayed childless as a consequence of understanding that where there is no self, there is no procreation in the image of. Medea didn't get the memo, and took her role as *the* high priestess too seriously and too personally. She should have tried shapeshifting...

In mundane practice and parlance, entering 'no self' has the consequence of natural relaxation, the opposite of anxiety. The only condition is to remember a few obvious remarks: all that which we call success is the discursive language of a constituted process of comparison, not reality. All that which we call depression is language according to the labels of diagnosis, not reality. All that which we call madness is the language we impose on a process of privileged selection, not reality. All that which we call love is the language of desire, with desire in turn being constituted by words. If you simply remember to distance yourself from all points of identification, distancing yourself also from becoming involved with what is observed, be that the conceptual mind, or the body internalizing both intellect and emotion – then you can live happily ever after.

Now, what are the implications of this for the way in which we give voice to experience? The answer to this question is given in the gaze that's capable of tonal awareness. What we find in the act of distancing, what underlies its structure, is a form of watching, a form of vigilance over just what and how language defines and constitutes our reality. And yet, while the body participates in watching itself thinking, it's not always the case that the thinking subject is actually aware of this process of watching, hence the false fantasy identifications with whatever happens to befall the mind. But we may get a glimpse into how this works, when we catch ourselves asking: 'did I hear that right?' 'is what I saw – loud and clear too – what I think it is?' 'what is this hearing and seeing simultaneously all about exactly?'

Similarly, how many of us can say, 'I fell in love because of watching, because my eyes fell into my mouth, the door to my desiring and burning gut, I am thus bewitched?' What is this fire exactly? Do we have a problem with precision here? We have words, plenty of them, but how exact are they, really?

Freud developed some solid thoughts on the event of voyeurism experienced as trauma. Children tend to lose their voices if they happen to surprise their parents in sexual intercourse. As he rightly observed in his writing about the primal scene, the witnessing act itself goes on to manifest as an interpretation of violence and sexual excitement at the same time. If this interpretation is insisted upon, acquiring new facets every time, thus becoming compulsive, it gives rise to psycho-pathology, to muteness or babble, or oracular voice that disturbs the general code for cultural preconditioning.

In his letter to Wilhelm Fliess in 1887 Freud mentions the term *urszene* for the first time, speculating also on how old children are when they are liable to 'hear things' that they would understand only 'subsequently' in six or seven months.[6] I would suggest here that what Freud was really interested in was timbre, the voice in the head, resonating images and their changing modulations to the point of confusion: 'What *did* I hear, exactly?'

The movement here is how to get the child, or the woman in love, for that matter, to traverse the space between experiencing fantasy as a point of identification with the self to enunciating: 'I am not my fantasy, there is no anchoring in the body of this fantasy. This fantasy has no referential point.' In the language of psychotherapy this line makes a lot of sense, but it's bad news for business. *No self* presupposes nothing to fix. If there's nothing to fix, there can be no theories. Freud liked to write a lot. Analyze, reflect, evaluate and pass judgment. He was no Zen Buddhist either, where such radical ideas of acceptance are a commonality. I can imagine his bafflement. Similarly, what does it mean for a woman in love to realize that if she gazes into love, it is herself she gazes into, not the object of her desire? While I'm not a dancer, I like to perform what I imagine are answers to true questions. Here's an image from such a performance, when I played with gazes Medea style.

There's a significant moment in Pasolini's take on the discourse on desire in *Medea*, when Jason, Medea's treacherous lover, insists that the only reason why she ever went with him, denying in the process her crucial help with stealing the Golden Fleece, is because she wanted his body. Medea is speechless at such an accusation, and urges Jason not to boast about it. But how does she then compensate for this loss of language? When this loss is not resolved other than through losing some more, the desired man's body included, Medea goes back to her magic, above words and rational discourse. She issues powerful visualizations that kill Jason's new bride, formulates clear curses on Jason's life, and takes the lives of their children. Well, that actually makes a lot of sense in the modern society that likes to keep its priorities straight.

If Medea fails to come to terms with Jason's rejection of her love — culturally speaking, for spiritually, in the sense of embodying the 'unnaturalness of the gods,' this failure is more like success — then it's because she forgets to inquire into the nature of Jason's truth, which is related to the trivial pursuit of an erect cock. While Jason has no trouble reducing himself to what drives his lower guts, Medea sees such a reduction as a personal affront to her magical powers. Had she tried to localize where exactly in her own body Jason's insult could be found, she might have ended up with a relaxing sigh, rather than a mad cry. We find that what Medea lost in her transition from the archaic society of her people to the modern one of Jason's is this wisdom: just as there is no self that goes before its name, nor is there any love that goes beyond its construct.

I would venture here to add to what Freud was speculating on and suggest that the psycho-pathological response to the primal scene, or any other scene that leaves us speechless, is a response that recognizes a grand void: the zero point where the self meets love to have a fantasy affair, the child meets his mother to fuck her, and the woman meets her man to give him language.

If we stay with this possibility for a moment, we can then say that what unleashes the interpretation of the act of love as violence and excitement is not the sudden awareness, or even meta-awareness of there being a self watching what is happening, but rather the sudden experience of the dissolution of the self, where the self realizes that it is part of everything and nothing at the same time. The self that goes through the doors of a new perception, to use this very apt cliché here, goes blissful before it panics.

When panic occurs – for it will occur – 'oh my god, I've lost my self, now what?' – the subject has two options, to forget or to remember: to remember that there's relation and hence connectedness, or to forget and hence cling to past projections where the self still enjoys the privileges of the ego that raises itself to the status of savior, general defender, and champion.

Culturally this response has been stamped or rather, negotiated and transacted with as shame: 'Thou shall not watch, or covet another man's woman,' the Bible instructs us, and lo and behold, we find this very line informing many a premise for psychoanalytical practice: 'There is shame in the world. Shame is bad. Let's get rid of shame. But.' What do we find in the but(t) – pardon the pun? The act of riddance that threatens us with more displaced demons? The guilt demon must be fed too, in the same old room with mirror doors, with no chance for lamentation – lamentation having been banished from the civilized world.

Again, in the final scene in *Medea,* Jason yells desperately: 'Give me my children's bodies, so I can bury them.' Medea says, 'No. Nothing is possible any more.' Then the curtain goes down. For Medea the fire that she has prepared for herself and her children becomes a replacement for the lost voice of loss. She is not interested in Jason's culture. For her, the only truth that remains is the fire sounding loss, giving voice to it. When she says *no,* what she says *no* to is language, Jason's language shaming her. In his own lamentation, we all hear clearly what is always implicit in culture, culture's weapon against its subjects: shame and guilt. We hear it loud and crisp: 'what have you done woman, have you no shame, can you at least feel guilty, a little remorseful, please?' Medea says, 'No.'

But this is Medea, the bereaved mother, who says *no.* Medea, the childless witch, survives beyond the lamentation: 'nothing is possible any more.' The reason for this has to do with the man asking the wrong question. What is implied in his attitude of shaming is that once assumptions are made on the premise of entitlement, then indeed, nothing is possible any more – except for the woman to remember her wisdom of connecting to the state before naming occurs in the form of the first person pronoun.

85

Maria Callas, *the* name over all the names in the opera world, even now, died childless, after having enchanted the world with her presence. Pasolini also died childless, his murder still unresolved. Shapeshifters, blazing and breezing through the world of conventions, setting the bar high for the immeasurable potential.

I don't know if Euripides intended his play to function as a cautionary tale: 'don't tempt the childless witch' – as a literary critic, I'm not even interested in the author's intention – but I like to think that such a caution is embedded in the narrative, especially between the points of *yes* and *no*. In Pasolini's sublime rendition, we find a very well calibrated tonal timbre in the eyes of the protagonists, in their body-language and costumes, and in their unresolved ambivalence as to what is best to flirt with: nature or culture. Some would say, it's natural for a woman to have children, until we hear God yell at Eve: 'if you absolutely *had* to be so stupid, desiring to fix it too' – though, indeed, what has stupidity got to do with it?

Whatever the case, God cursed Eve in the story that still has a major impact on many. But she speaks back. The minute Eve stops to ponder and ask, 'I wonder why God prohibited us from enjoying all the fruits in the garden?' is the minute when the Snake wins, when philosophy wins. From here, there's a short path from wonderment to full blown inquiry. The only thing missing is the words. A true question starts with finding the words to say it. If childless women have appeared throughout the ages as witches, it's because some stopped asking the lamenting question, 'why me, why must it be me suffering from infertility?' posing instead a better question, one that's initiated by the same spell of astonishment that perhaps Eve was under, 'I wonder why childless women are prohibited from staying childless, if they so wished?' Then the words of rejection, of speaking back and against the orders that make no space for the 'anomalous' category. We are precisely not with the cultural ultimatum, 'either you have children or you don't, and if you don't you get punished for it.' No. We're here with the spell of the woman who can both pose and answer true questions, thus situating herself at the midpoint. 'If I so wish, I'll say no...'

The language of the oracle starts with this speaking back, with the clear articulation of this negation, but the voice is more than that of echoing the patriarchs who dictate: 'an eye for an eye.' The childless witch finds it infinitely more interesting to probe the realm beyond mere imitation, where 'an eye for an eye' could translate into the idea of 'a curse for a curse.' It's more fun to play with the immutable justice, than with laws that are ever changing according to whoever gets to decide in whatever name they fancy.

Many cultures use an anthropomorphic idiom to characterize mentally unstable people. We refer to them as cuckoos. I often wondered why we say that. What is there in the cuckoo's cry that is not orderly already? I try to imagine Medea sounding like the cuckoo. Callas was good at imitating this bird, but Pasolini wouldn't let her sing...

1   See *The Greek Plays: Sixteen Plays by Aeschylus, Sophocles, and Euripides* (Modern Library Classics, 2017).

2   See the screenplay interpretation, rather than an adaptation of Euripides' *Medea*, by Pier Paolo Pasolini, 1969. *Medea* is directed by Pier Paolo Pasolini with the screenplay featuring Italian and English subtitles; director of photography, Ennio Guarnieri; editor, Nino Baragli; produced by Franco Rossellini; a Euro-International-Janus Films production; distributed by New Lino Cinema. Running time: 100 minutes.

3   Most biographers of Maria Callas are reluctant to write about Callas' presumed abortion, as it's not something that can be verified, though Arianna Stassinopoulos Huffington states in her bestselling book: *Maria Callas: The Woman Behind the Legend* that Callas regretfully aborted her pregnancy at the insistence of her longtime lover, Aristotle Onassis (1981: 287, Simon and Schuster). The tabloid press is full of rumors and wild stories, but all one can do is speculate. It remains unlikely, however, that the 42-year old career woman would get pregnant out of the blue with her lover of almost 10 years already. Her strained relationship with her mother, a much spoken about topic, makes it also even more unlikely to believe that Callas had any real interest in changing her status from childless to mother.

4   See Anne Carson's essay, 'The Gender of Sound' from *Glass, Irony, and God* (New Directions, 1992: 121).

5   See *The Greek Plays: Sixteen Plays by Aeschylus, Sophocles, and Euripides* (Modern Library Classics, 2017).

6   See *The Standard Edition of the Complete Psychological Works of Sigmund Freud*, Vol. 1. p. 247 (1953, The Hogarth Press).

Oracle

Imagine the woman who says: 'I've said what I wanted to say,' and goes and lives her life without a thought about having to explain further, or having a sense that she needs to explain more because somehow she owes it to the others to do so. Now imagine taking this vision on the realization plane. Can you see it happen? If you can't, what would it take for you to get past the incredulity that saying, 'I've said what I wanted to say,' can actually occur in your mundane life? Have you ever even tried saying, 'I've said what I wanted to say?' If you did try saying this, did your words have major impact? I insist on the 'major' part, simply because, if you ask me, I can tell you that I said, 'I've said what I wanted to say,' many times to little effect, and more as a result of resigning to the futility of the conditions I've said this under, with resentment as a primary tone. Not the best of states, when you want to assert in earnest what you think is your personal justice.

Just take a brief moment to contemplate on how you hear this line, 'I've said what I wanted to say,' whether you said it yourself or not. Is the voice you hear the voice of negation or the voice of affirmation? It makes a difference. Now contemplate on the tonality and gravity that your words had in a time when you had to say something important. Contemplate until you fall into a trance. We need this trance to make a point about the oracular as it relates precisely to the childless witch and the kind of stories the childless witch participates in.

I often think of trance states and the use of the metaphor of going deep into something. Going deep into something presupposes operating with the linguistic awareness of space. We're with the basement here, and the dark. But as far as I can tell, exploring utter darkness kicks your sensorial experience to a heightened state, so we're not with the deep, the low. Butoh performers dance in the dark as part of their training. What visions do they have when they are sensorially deprived? A good question. But then again, if you ask me, I can easily get to a place of utter darkness while sitting right under the most glaring sun, and vice versa. Why? Because if I decide while in the sun that now I'm sitting in darkness, then it is so. My magic operates entirely with speech acts and linguistic awareness. The only training that I need revolves around a framing device for a story to emerge first and then get kicked to next level, whether we're with the metaphors pertaining to a high or low plane of narativization. In other words, what I'm saying that's not popular at all in 'spiritual' circles is that

I get in a trance state when I reduce the noise of what is generally perceived as a 'cool mystery.' There's no mystery. Just narrative. No ordeal. No drugs. No fasting. No incense. Just contemplation. I ask my mind, 'what stories should we now spin?' and the mind goes wild. My mind likes it very much when it gets to collaborate on the stories we create together, on command. Just as nothing is real and nothing has substance, so we, the mind and myself, don't get too excited about 'mysteries.' Note here that I dissociate my mind from the constructed 'I as a witness' on purpose. All things being equal, just as I don't want to fall pray to the stories my mind construes about my super sensual self as a body, I don't want to fall pray to the stories that the intellect is all there is either, because 'I can just feel it.' We are cognizant on more than one plane, in this case here that of the mind and the body. The setting and the landscape plays a role, and memory plays a role. Words mediate.

But let's ask this question first: what's going on when we are low or when we are high in a trance? We operate with the notion of 'high and low' here simply because this dichotomy is part of the register most people use when they refer to describing their personal experiences of being in a trance. The point is that you can actually only be in deep trance and at the same time also able to explore the base levels of the subconscious, if you're in a heightened state of perception *via a story*, which is the opposite of the idea of being in a haze or experiencing stupor, thus not responding to external stimuli, a definition prevalent in the discourse about trance states.[1] In other words, unless you use words to frame how you get into magic, there's no trance, not even when you happen upon a drum that you hear from afar when you accidentally stumble over one in your walking strolls in the sand by a beach.

We'll come back to the drum, but as a first example of how we frame *being* in an altered state of consciousness, I like to point to the martial artist's skill of placing himself in a trance state whenever he needs to enter his most vigilant posture. When *kenjutsu*, Iaido master Isao Machii has to split a bullet with his sword, what I see him doing is place himself in this very state of exploring utter darkness via framing a story in which he simply cuts the bullet, regardless of the conditions for cutting it – conditions that most mortals viewing the performance deem impossible. But here's the spiel: if he succeeds in cutting the bullet that's shot at him at high speed, it's not because he can see anything, but because he's in a trance ruled not by reverie, but rather, by rationalism. This rationalism expresses itself in the articulation of the desire to enact, in the moment it arises, the idea of being useful in a way that completely bypasses expectation. In other words, this Japanese master uses his body as a tool that he puts in the service of his story in exactly the same way we saw Carlotta Ikeda doing with her body.

So we're here with a story and a tool, a witch's essentials. Apart from my own childless body as a tool, I also work with cards. I even fancy the idea that since what I'm after is clarity, there's no difference between what I do and what a martial artist does when they shoot for precision. In my work with cartomancy and oracular language I'm fascinated by how we rationalize our different tactics for framing our motivations to perform an identity, a ritual, or a set of conventions, whether they are all transgressive or conservative. I'm interested in this especially since I deal with people who are quite miserable, simply because they move in the dark, unable to express how exactly they can render themselves useful.

Most people think that they can only be useful to others when they rise to some perceived expectations. What I'm interested in is how I can get people to experience being useful without thinking at the same time that their usefulness has to follow external demands. A tall order, as it requires focus that's based primarily on a process of discarding lulling thoughts. For instance, it's quite incredible that I actually know many young women who never question this expectation, namely that they get married and have children. Without taking partisan sides, if these girls knew better, they *could* ask questions, but as far as my observations are concerned they are all in a state of stupor: 'Mother did it, I also have to.'

Being in a state of stupor is not the same as being in the kind of trance that makes the martial artist achieve his goal. Yet the focus is not on how impossible it is really to split a bullet into halves while it flies right past you, but rather, on the act of cutting itself. Machii *sensei* is not thinking, 'wow, I have to cut this tiny thing at such high speed so that I can demonstrate it to the world that it's possible' – he holds many Guinness World Records for his *katana* skills[2]. Rather, what he's thinking is that he has to cut the thing. Period. That's the essential, to make the cut. Ability to make the cut beyond the regular physical training is not the essential. Demonstrating the act is not the essential either. What's essential is the cut itself. More essential even is how the *story* about cutting goes inside the head first at the level of the image. This awareness of just how visualization impacts is what makes the difference.

In a similar fashion, when I lay down the cards for clarity, what I always have an eye for is not on how big or small a problem is, or what kind of sleep of ignorance the person I'm reading the cards for is in. Rather, I'm interested in what is essentially the case. What is *not* the case has no interest to me. If cutting to the bone is the case, then anything else that presents itself besides that is a distraction. What can present itself is mostly clichés related to how we perform the job by adopting a position of privilege. Having empathy is one, exercising compassion is another. But here's what I say: if the diviner is to maintain focus, then the only sympathy that must be achieved is not the one between the diviner and the sitter, but the one between the diviner's own trance state of heightened 'seeing' in the dark and the act of cutting it to the bone. The sitter doesn't exist. Only the question exists.

I like to think of what I'm doing when reading the cards in terms of this relation of sympathy: Ashes to ashes. Dust to dust. Fire to fire. Water to water. Wind to wind. When thought of in these terms, no interpretation is too daunting, whether you look at two cards or twenty cards in a row. The movement will always be the same: split to split. 'Yes, but can the other handle the truth?' some may ask, enticing to being careful. But the way I see it is in this manner: I'm not in the care-giving business. I'm in the clarity business. Clarity has nothing to do with care. 'You're good at divining because you have no children to care for, and you work in the lineage of the childless witch,' someone once said to me. I thought about it, but I couldn't see the correlation.

This I know, however: keeping an eye on what's essential is my recipe for a good trance-inducing experience. It's not about going deep, letting yourself be enchanted or lulled by the voice of distraction, however whispering and soothing it may be. I myself have no patience for this kind of transmission: 'empower yourself, let go of yourself, go deeper into yourself.' As far as I'm concerned, a good trance is all about making my hairs stand, so I can split the hell out of the most invisible issue. I'm aided in this endeavor by my consistent practice of questioning, on the one hand, and on the other hand, by my practice of standing prepared so I can catch the obvious, or the spontaneous that arises. For instance, I ask myself: how can I place myself in a heightened state, where no word of culture is in sight? I imagine the childless witch being the kind of martial artist that makes herself fully useful when she lets no dictations inform her actions. The idea is to focus on the split and nothing but, to forget the words and remember the body, but only insofar as the body is a tool, not some holy totalitarian temple that supersedes the capacity to be crystal clear in the head. I put down some cards for this very question, just to demonstrate. Indeed, I got a visual message of the very idea, when I looked at the my Marseille tarot cards, here the Tower, the Queen of Coins, and the 5 Batons.

Blast the establishment and take sovereignty in your personal work. A smashed tower can be of more value towards a new spin. What can this be? I answer this question by posing another question: why do people go to the oracles? Because they're more honest. That is to say, more honest than the mainstream cultural dictations we're all accustomed to. That's the answer I give myself every time I actually pose that question. Which is often, as I'm in the business of checking with what I'm thinking and what I'm doing all the time.

The oracle is a thing of threads, weaving. Fiber versus the womb. The body as a tool against all our complaints about how our mothers fucked us up. Here's what I learned from practicing martial arts, and that includes watching countless Japanese TV films, from historical, samurai drama to romantic comedies: when you're honest, you stop complaining. I'm quite convinced in my childless days that the reason why I'm utterly content with my lot is because of the time when I realized that living others' life was not the way forward. But how to do this, without appearing merely as a recalcitrant teen, who thinks her revolution is different than that of the world? Entitlement without a just cause for it discloses nothing but a complete lack of distinction. That wasn't the life I was interested in living. So I started getting Zen, as it were, and concomitantly reading and watching films, French *film noir* to begin with. As my tastes got more refined, I shifted to Japanese aesthetics. Since then, there's been no turning back.

THE VOICE AND THE PULSE

I got into Maya Deren films and work because of her third husband, Japanese composer Teiji Itō, 18 years her junior. Although they were married for just one year until her death in 1961, childless and at age of 44, they were together for several more, years in which they created short films, while experiencing also being possessed by the Haitian Vodou gods. Not exactly your New York bohemian setting, a scene they were part of. Maya Deren, dancer, choreographer, avant-garde filmmaker, film theorist, ethnographer, anthropologist, and

'Russian Jew' *par excellence*, meets musician, one into scores and tunes, drum beats and orchestrations. A romantic story. According to Teiji Itō, 'Maya was always a Russian. In Haiti she was a Russian. She was always dressed up, talking, speaking many languages and being a Russian.'[3] A composer would be interested in the sounds different languages make...

Deren was a polyglot, a woman of high energy, and, according to her own admission, dedicated to the sea and dreams. Although she was interested in the intricacies of the mind, she viewed her own expansiveness from a scientific point of view. That is to say, Deren was a woman of experiments, and as such, a woman of her age, some would argue. The only difference is that whereas her experiments were carried out in the name of scientific knowledge, Deren's prolific output was primarily done in the name of the oracular, that which resists interpretation. Other critics might call this particular manifestation of the oracular 'discovery,' and thus align it with methods that lead to knowledge, but I prefer seeing what Deren did as a manifestation of favoring the straight oracular to the merely scientific pursuit that blends curiosity with observation, deriving knowledge from processing information.

Any moment spent in Maya Deren's company, when we watch her films or read her words, discloses plenty evidence towards demonstrating how she developed her interests in surrealist stories, Freudian theories of the symbol, gestalt psychology, and African spiritualities, especially as far as the oracular is concerned. Deren wasn't just interested in what the mind has to say, what the gods have to say, or what a symbol has to say that necessitates decoding. Rather, she was interested in the poetic message, that is to say, the kind of message that swerves from the mainstream understanding of cultural symbols, or more specifically, from understanding what art communicates. While the symbolic is given primacy in her works, the idea is not to make the viewer or the reader follow an instruction: 'here's the surrealist element,' or 'here's the occult idea.' 'Interpret.' Yet merely pointing to the ambiguous in oracular visual language is not the most interesting. What is more interesting is what the oracular has to say about how we communicate the necessity to serve and be served directly on the mundane, not the sacred level.

In her celebrated anthropology work, *Divine Horsemen: The Living Gods of Haiti* (1953), Deren makes it clear that Haitian spirituality is not based on belief, but rather on the question of how well gods and men serve one another. As the condition for mutual and beneficial serving is a strong psyche, children, for instance, are barred from the possibility to be under spirit possession. They may participate in the Vodou rituals, whose aim is precisely that, possession in a trance state, but it's considered a bad omen to be ridden by a god if one is not well past adolescence.[4]

Now, the reason why I include Maya Deren in my contemplations of childlessness is because of her overall emphasis on the non-collaborative in all acts of communication. Culturally speaking, as a child is used as currency for what adults want to communicate about their usefulness in society, the child is thus considered as a vehicle towards maintaining the symbolic value associated with status and privilege. Deren comes along and questions the usefulness of the presupposed collaboration between society and family. As people put children into the world with view to maintaining the species, society rewards them a with a golden egg, or the promise for the Garden of Eden, where everyone can enjoy the benefits of culture, including being free from the pesky snakes, seducing with their lies about the value of knowing better. Consensus reality is created under the banner, 'ignorance is bliss.'

Deren didn't think she needed children in order to communicate her art or her usefulness, although she dreamed of writing a children's book on dance. In an essay published posthumously on the art of filmmaking, 'Amateur versus Professional,' Deren makes the case of discarding all collaborative efforts in favor of using one's own mobile body as a subject, prop, or other theatrical device, the imaginative mind, and the freedom to use both.[5] One sees the same nerve at work in her fascination and study of not only her own body, but also that of others, especially when they are put in the service of creating an experience. Fiber and texture are the focus.

For Deren, the ultimate art is not simply to just record experiences, as experiences happen by default, but look at how they are created. In filmmaking, if the cameraman is the seeing eye, the cutter, the editor of the shots, is the creator of the experience of what the camera records. In a similar fashion, in ritual dance or the experience of spirit possession, the collaboration on how an experience is created is not between people as a spiritual community and what each person brings to the table, but rather between the individual person as a visionary and his or her capacity to enunciate what merits attention. What do the gods say? What does the oracular say when all reliance on second-guessing is eradicated? How do men create their experience of immediacy? How do women create their experience of waiting? Deren saw men and women as being different in their attitudes precisely towards the constructedness of immediacy and waiting, granting women strength on account of their capacity to 'wait nine months for the concept of a child.'[6] The child as an idea is the construction of the default experience of being pregnant with a child. It is within this distinction that we begin to realize how the conceptual participates in the construction of all emotional, physical, and mental states.

Maya Deren's art is significant because it says something about how women internalize their 'being in the world' on a premise of hearing their own pulse and listening to their own voices. In other words, women can dance to the tune of their own ability to wait even for the stories that they see unfolding before their eyes, or take shape as an idea first. If men are good at recording an idea, women are good at editing. Editing is made of cuts. Cutting to the essential, to the bone. If a woman decides to cut the idea of children out of her motion picture, she is a already an artist by Deren's standards, an artist who thinks, and because she thinks, she is able to pose true questions. 'Who am I having children for?' is *the* question that informs the childless witch's nerve and fiber, taking place in a cradle that's made up of threads and tightropes. One doesn't give birth. One weaves instead, creating the experience of fate as an oracular story, away from prescribed traditions and set dictations.

ENTANGLEMENTS

Two of Maya Deren's films make explicit use of the idea of entanglements, nets, and textures: her most famous work, *Meshes of the Afternoon* (1943) made with her second husband, Alexander Hamid, a Czech photographer and filmmaker, and her unfinished work, *The Witch's Cradle* (1944), with artist Marcel Duchamp. Both films operate with passages that are textured and movement through these passages. Both films make use of the figure of the labyrinth, with the motif of the thread interchanging between meshes and veils that are woven and lines that are crossed to form a design akin to a spider's web. The oracular is represented as always being on the other side, yet easily accessible through 'controlled accidents,' a notion Deren developed in her filmmaking theories.

Now, what interests me here is not so much what the films say, as they follow quite standard conventions for art photography and cinematography, where the motif of exclusive body parts looms large, and we go from medium to long and close-up shots of feet, hands, or lips. Rather what's interesting is the controlled incoherence that's tied, literally in a way, by a red thread. For instance, in *Meshes of the Afternoon*, a protagonist – Maya Deren herself – enters a house and falls asleep in a chair. She starts dreaming. First a hand appears in a road delivering a poppy flower, *the* sleep inducing plant. Then we have a chasing scene in which a black cloaked figure whose face is a mirror is being followed by the protagonist. The camera zooms in on the feet and their sound on ground, pavement, and stairs.

The dream features the same elements that started the dream, that is, the scene when the woman enters that house, but not before she almost accidentally loses the key that opens the door to the house. After some fiddling with the key, the woman heads to a comfortable armchair, whose upholstery features flowers. She sits in it, and closes her eyes. We're now with the world of the somniferous, sleep inducing pulse. The almost lost key appears in the dream, coming out of the woman's mouth. Alongside it, a knife. The knife first appears in her hands. Next we have a play of hands over a table, with a palm stretched, holding the key in a gesture that invites us to think of the game in which we have to guess what people hold in their closed fists. Here we're with the reveal.

'The reveal' – let's call it that because it's significant – functions on different planes of perception, suggesting that what we're dealing with here is not so much the world of a surrealist dreamer invested in the language of symbols, but rather, the world of a magician invested in the game of prestige. For instance, a stage magician whose trick specialty is sleight-of-hand goes through three steps towards ultimate enchantment: first, there's the pledge, when the magician shows you something that holds the promise for an extraordinary feat. Second, there's the turn of the trick, when the magician makes his promise disappear as it were; now you see the rabbit coming out of the hat, and now you don't. Third, there's the prestige, when the magician demonstrates his ultimate skill, which is about making things disappear and then re-appear miraculously, especially after the viewer has been convinced that such a thing is impossible.

I've read many analyses of Maya Deren's films, but not a single one of them pointed to this obvious aspect in her work, namely that what she's interested in is clear perception, not the rendition of a constructed experience as a symbolic manifestation of unconscious desires.[7] If one reads the biographical literature closely, we also learn that although Deren's father was a psychiatrist, and she herself was well versed in Freudian theories and psychoanalysis, we also notice that what her work articulates is a departure from investigating into the tripartite structure of the mind divided into the conscious/subconscious/unconscious categories.[8] While Deren gives Freud a nod, she finds chance, the oracular, and the controlled accident, also known as randomness, infinitely more interesting, precisely because the unpredictable can occur with maximum impact on all three 'Freudian' levels, not just the merely symbolic manifest in the unconscious, or the merely conscious, manifest in the concrete.

As far as I'm concerned, *Meshes of the Afternoon* can be understood in terms of the oracular, when the oracular holds the key to what can be cut to the essentials. There's more prestige in how enchantment holds the key to solving a mystery, than in how a theory forces a solution through to fit its enunciation. In *Meshes of the Afternoon* it is suggested that the male lover in the film stabs the woman to death in her dream. Where the key opens and closes for the flow of experiences, the knife cuts the possibility to have an issue. That is to say, there's no issue from this relationship, as in, no children.

Where the gift of communicating a message clearly is concerned we can argue in favor of Deren's brilliance. There's no shallow thinking in her output, whether visual or verbal. Every idea is turned over on all its facets, before it comes to full expression. In her writings, while Deren may often come across as opinionated, upon finer analysis it's hard to find evidence that would support the idea that her opinions are not informed. For they are. And more so. Deren knows how to use her thread, the key she holds in her palm, and the knife she lends to her lovers.

Maya Deren's entanglements can be said to function like an hour-glass vertical labyrinth, with the sand running out through different openings, some grains remaining locked blocking the false exit. What I personally find striking in her art is her ability to deflect the viewer's attention from what is otherwise shown. For instance, while the viewer gets busy with the urge to interpret immediately the symbols that present themselves in a strange sequence, something else takes place in plain view that's not incoherently fragmentary. For instance, there's strong emphasis on feet running through sand or a dusty road, leaving heavy imprints behind. If we're looking for the oracular, I suggest we find it in these traces.

In Deren's art we're not with an emphasis on interpretation — as in, 'guess what this key means?' — but rather with ritual. The oracular is in the gesture itself, in the stepping on it. Magic resides in the soles of your feet. This tactic of constructing an experience via revealing the prestige by way of stepping on perception itself reminds me of what Carlotta Ikeda said in an interview, when asked whether she was interested in developing a way of training butoh dancers. She said, no. If she ever had to say anything, however, she'd ask dancers to consider the practical study of the sole of their feet, how they step on it, and how they carry their weight around.[9] Her students often report that if she ever needed to get a sense of a person's capacity, she'd simply ask them to jump. Most dancers would thus think that what Ikeda was after was to assess the quality of the jump. But rather, what she was after was the landing, the imprint of their feet in the ground.

Such an approach to life and art doesn't require interpretative skills — though it helps to be able to decode a text, or the world around you, to reflect on it, analyze it and offer an evaluation. But in our context here what's more important for the women who didn't have an issue with not having any issue from their relationships is the idea of constant discovery.

My favorite among Deren's films is the one in which she gets washed on the beach and then runs around with chess pieces in her hands. *At Land* (1944) is very much a manifestation of the direct experience of landing, both horizontally, and also on your feet. The same techniques of deflection are in place here as in her other works, with the informed viewer being prone to jumping at interpreting symbols, rather than simply just jumping with Maya, the character, on whatever she steps on. As the sea makes its continuous motion of push and pull, with the waves ebbing and flowing, rising and receding, we're meant to consider this continuum against the background of play, unpredictability, and risk.

At Land features chess players who are, however, not very dedicated. Two women play chess on the beach where Deren's character has just been rolling out of the sea. The focus is not on the chessboard. The focus is on chatter, words. We don't hear any of it, as this is a silent movie, but there's animated and vivid movement of the mouths. Deren approaches the scene, and observes. Then she takes hold of the women's heads, and in a caressing movement she offers them gentle strokes of their hair. The two are enthralled, but they don't stop talking. As they don't pay attention, Deren snatches some chess pieces, and starts running with them. No one follows her. Although their game was interrupted, with chess pieces now gone missing, the two are unaffected. They don't realize that what has been stolen from them is the words themselves. They have all been plucked.

I find this film most powerful precisely in this, if my creative interpretation holds, in the idea that while we always operate according to the rules of the game, when we lose focus on just how we put two and two together, the sea and its monsters come to wash us out of our existence. Deren's character landed in the middle of the game, as it were, and we go from one party to another, both informed by people yakking. It's a relief that we don't hear their voices. But we can 'hear' Deren's feet, and the imaginary sound of her slithering of her body across the long table where many are seated for dinner, drinks, and a game of chess. Yet as in the previous scene, no one sees her occupying their space. They have their empty words to care about.

As the film ends with footprints in the sand, we're left with the idea of possession. Once left in the sand, who do these footprints belong to? Who can they possess in turn? As they lose specificity, going translucent with the sand and the sea, perhaps we can think of these footprints as Deren's offerings to the sea goddess. In her films, whenever there's a gathering — her film *Ritual* best represents crowds at a party — what we're dealing with is not the idea of community, the idea of artist collaboration, but rather, the idea of how an individual functions psychologically at the level of what is perceived precisely as part of a ritual of dispossession.

The gathering itself is the Minotaur's labyrinth, and hence something to fear, as sacrifices are made here. Ariadne comes along *as* an individual, and plots a way out of it using thread.

In other words, the message is not that it's warm and cozy in the womb. Rather, the message is that once washed out of the womb, there can only be a party of one, with the movement taking place between states of being possessed (by name, identity, masks, and marks), and being dispossessed (and thus a god landed in you as a manifestation of the sea).

How do you land? Are your feet strong enough? These are the questions that the childless witch poses. These questions are oracular in their thrust, precisely because few pose them ingeniously. As most are busy talking themselves to death, what is *the* saving grace symbol for everything? Children. Poor children... I want to sympathize, but since I'm not in the business of passing judgment on what others find meaningful in life, I'll just say that where true questions are concerned, what we need more of is the brutality of clear vision. What we need less of is to waste our time on prioritizing the irrevocably inessential in the name of mythologizing on the reproductive role of the woman.

KNOWING WHAT YOU DON'T KNOW THAT YOU KNOW

I posed this question earlier: 'why do people go to the oracles?' To know things. Especially the things that they can't bring to the consecrated tables of the professionals — by professionals I mean the group of people with degrees in psychology, psychiatry, psycho-therapy, and social work.

The interesting about a fortuneteller, a Zen master, a Tarot consultant, an astrologer, a Vodou priest, or an artist whose focus is ritual and the sacred, is that they are all invested in the knowing of things, especially the knowing of things on the plane that has less epistemology in it. Although some in this lot act on a premise of certitude while others don't, the latter being more open to accepting randomness and probability as a decisive factor in the passing of judgment on what is observed as phenomena via the tools engaged (cards, stars, sutras, or chickens), what they have in common is a shared acceptance of not knowing how they *do* know that they *know*. That is to say, it's not uncommon to hear a fortuneteller or a Zen master saying that they are fine with not knowing *how* exactly they know what they know. Now, this attitude runs counter to what we like to think of as clarity, as it's quite easy to infer that if you have clarity about something, then you also know what causes this clarity. But there's no correlation.

As someone who has built an entire academic career on how we know things, what we must pay for this knowledge, and what we use it for, I can safely say that I'm *not* fine with not knowing how I know what I know. It's a challenge for me to not be able to account for the source of my analogies. At the same time, as a diviner, or as someone who is invested in observing how the obvious manifests, I'm perfectly fine with not knowing anything about how I know that *this* is obvious.

It's in this, the manifestation of the obvious right under my assuming nose, that I find my work with the cards fantastic, insofar as I use the cards as a buffer precisely against the potential obsession with knowing. When things become interesting is at the point when I enchant myself and others with a form of knowing that exceeds the standard going about it, a procedure based on identifying causal relations: you understand that something happens because this something else happens. Yet going through life and always seeking understanding of causal relations is not only trite, but rather tiresome too in the long run. That 'this happens because of this other thing' presupposes giving a lot of attention to separations: 'me against the world, me against my lover, me against my self-image, me against my work, me against my health.' The list positing adversarial relations is long.

But knowing is more than knowing how causality works, and how it impacts on our lives. This 'more' is what I call self-enchantment. This 'more' is the bravery of honesty. The questions to pose here are these ones: how do we allow for other modes of knowing to be seated in us as 'more,' to use a metaphor from Vodou spirituality? To what extent are we fine with not knowing that we *do* know what we know? In psychoanalysis this state is identified with the unconscious that manifests itself as a form of heretic knowledge, as the unconscious is not subject to conscious control. Others point to the presence of a shadow self that just *knows* things, often of a disturbing character. While there's some truth to this territory supposedly populated by all that which is not culturally sanctioned or endorsed, I'm not in the camp of the enthusiasts who see the work of acknowledging the unconscious or the shadow – if that can even be done – as a solution to everything. I only find replacing mainstream culture with occult culture entertaining at best. At worst, participating in validating transgressions has consequences, as not everything we end up giving ourselves permission to do is beneficial to anyone, not even our own good self. From a psycho-therapy point of view, I have as yet to see selfishness solve anything.

Therefore I insist on this aspect of posing questions in relation to what we don't know that we do know from an explicit and direct, rather than implicit and gray angle, especially since I come across being confronted with what is often an indignation: 'how do you know that you don't want children in your life?' My answer, 'I don't know *how* I know it, but the knowledge itself is enough' baffles every time. This makes me think of what is at stake in the knowledge that the childless woman possesses, as it's quite bewitching. Here's what I have observed that makes the childless woman experience a shift to the other label, 'the childless witch.' It starts with how knowledge is transacted with and on what plane.

KNOWLEDGE AS ENCHANTMENT

The first thing that I note about the childless witch is that knowing – whether defined as ontological, epistemological, or metaphysical – is seated in her as a perpetual enchantment.

This manifests in the following way: the childless witch is capable of learning without words, that is to say, the woman has already internalized what the conceptual is all about: words as fictions. Because of this realization, the childless witch can let her *unselfconsciousness* lead the way. This can be translated along three propositions:

[1] The childless witch is susceptible to her environment to the point that she can breathe it through her skin. In other words, the woman has vision and clarity that are not informed by guilt and self-pity: 'oh, you don't have any children, what a shame...'

Getting to this susceptibility requires some work on detaching from investing attention in worrying about the public opinion about being a childless visionary enchantress, aka 'a witch.' If you read these words and nod, 'I don't give a flying fuck about the public opinion,' I congratulate you. You have graduated to knowing the value of your own skin in th game. But if you have the tiniest reservation, I invite you to consider where exactly your attention goes, and why. In other words, consider the idea that the childless witch is susceptible to the workings of her own mind too.

[2] The childless witch is open to working with the present, even when she is in the business of invoking ancestors, doing necromantic work, drumming with the Vodou priests, or divining from the ancient memory of her gut.

The childless witch knows that Hekate won't just pick her folk, simply because they happen to like spending time at the crossroads in the wilderness at midnight, or acting along with Maria Callas when she impersonates Medea, Hekate's foremost priestess. For instance, you might like to know that I once engaged in all sorts of rituals to get Hekate to be my patron. She said no. Every time. And I went, wtf? Every time. Did she care about my being appalled at her rejection? She didn't. How did I know that she didn't care about my efforts? I have no idea. But as part of the concluding ritual, the answer was always no. Since divination with the Tarot cards is what I do when I transact with my 'self' in magical setting, I heed attention when I get the Tower card four times in row. In my example here, I simply concluded that being in Hekate's temple was not in the cards for me.

Since I'm also a 'card person' to the bones and beyond my soul because I like semiotics and the poetic language of the visual text, every time I perform any kind of magic, I check with the cards from this perspective as well, that is to say, the perspective of the academic who formally analyzes an image. I allow, however, for my susceptibility to be part of my coherence and rhythm. This means that I'm quite gleeful about knowing things in advance, including not knowing how I just know things, even before I get any cards on the table. But as it happens, and since I'm very much invested in the construction of the experience of analysis via deduction and via observing how the obvious emerges from the visual text, what I actually do is just ask for confirmation. For instance, I love teasing the cards by asking them to confirm the presence of spirit at the crossroads. As it happens, in my occult conjuring the ones who show up are Legba, the Vodou gatekeeper loa, and Lucifer, the light-bringer. When I ask the cards, and that in spite of my knowing it already, they confirm it every time without error: the Fool shows up in questions about Legba, and the Charioteer shows up when Lucifer and I have some nice business to attend to. When I say every time, I mean just that: every time. It's almost as if there's an internal drum inside of me, and when I beat it, I enter a trance. When I tell others about it, they go, 'whoa, that's goddamn good magic.' It's good magic because I use my body and visualization capacity to enchant myself beyond what we call ordinary perception. In other words, my occult leaning is entirely dependent on how I frame whatever story I need to enter.

Now, from the point of view of storytelling in magical time, the childless witch knows that if she does this, ask the cards to confirm what she already knows, she must pay a price. In this part of the story when the cards are on the table and when we assign agency to the cards, we can say that the cards don't like being tested, and they take what you do as a sign of your not being serious. Think about it: the cards have a point. What do you need all that confirmation for, when you already got your signs at the moment of your invocation at the crossroads?

As you don't want to offend the gods of divination, you must think of ways of using the cards as spell work, or as a ritual instead, whenever you ask for such a trite thing as confirmation. That's the payment in the form of more work, but it's a also a payoff. There's nothing like the feeling of placing yourself in a position that's beyond all settled negotiation. While we can quickly agree that either you know things, or you don't, we can also agree that clarity is not something you switch on and off. Zen masters could testify to this, so the idea is to go beyond having to decide. The idea that your shadow knows more than you do is a nice story, but from the perspective of continuous clarity, it's a bad story, for the shadow goes exactly nowhere. Therefore let us now move on to point three in this story, because there's such a thing as actuality in our fictional truths, and this one is never shady.

[3] The childless witch is always ready to know the facts. And here's the surprise. The only fact we can all know is the fact of our name. Right here and right now. A name that we can also change any time. What the childless witch knows above all is that every thought populating her head is pure fiction, and that her act is that of the stage magician who pledges to show, then turns the trick of invisibility upside down, only to reveal the prestige in the end. 'It's here again. You can have it now. You're empowered. But not because I say so. *Pax vobiscum.*' You may enjoy enormously the realm of your imagination, but as thoughts come and go, they are just that, impermanent, always telling transitory stories.

Here I'd argue that the childless witches I've been referring to so far have all this in common: they are adept at self-enchantments as part of their knowing that detachment is the condition for the existence of all magic, or what I like to call 'the gift of fiction' one can give oneself, the gift of the controlled accident, as Deren would have it, or the gift of jumping into the void and leaving an imprint, if it were up to Carlotta Ikeda. Zohar Fresco would score the invisible notes and then drum to an impossible beat, while Callas as Medea would give herself the fiction of once more being *the* childless witch, serving and honoring Hekate.

The basic idea here is that once you know that every god-damn thought in your head is fantasy and fiction – and that includes love and hate, desire and fear – you're free. As you can actually sense yourself breathing – the only fact you will ever know beyond doubt – you realize that you can perform magic of the highest. This magic is of the highest for the simple reason that it is completely free of 'personal' involvement. Since the highest magic is always free, it takes an artful approach to attain it. As with all art, the starting point is the formulation of a true question. Once you have this fact in your hand, or head, namely, that all is fiction whose construction is subject to questioning, then you can go back to 'knowing' how you can be susceptible to your world in the best possible way, while also knowing how you can make yourself available to connecting with spirit. Now you may want to ask: 'what is self-enchantment exactly?' In response, I'd have to ask you back: 'have you listened at all to what I've been saying so far?'

Since we're with the oracular voice here, let's assume that the cards know best. Let us pose this question to the cards too, for they have a way of testing just how brave you are in the face of having to admit that you *do* know what you know, beyond theories of how powerful your unconscious is, how efficient your shadow is, or how mythical your dance. Look at these cards: the Sun, the Empress, and the Hermit:

I'd say the following: self-enchantment is happiness that's shared. It's brilliant and genuine empowerment. It's standing alone, inquiring into the nature of your mind and its illuminations. Can you sense the marvelous void? Your infinity? If you can't, imagine what Maya Deren might say, or some other childless witch you may know or have encountered.

1   See *Spirit Possession and Trance. New Interdisciplinary Perspectives.* Continuum Advances in Religious Studies, 6. Edited by Bettina E. Schmidt and Lucy Huskinson (Continuum 2010).

2   Read the interview, Sakura-Con 2017 - Isao Machii Interview that details some of the techniques that Isao Machii uses in his school [https://www.japanaradio.com/node/83 – last accessed on December 15, 2020]

3   In Maria Pramaggiore's essay: 'Performance and Persona in the U.S. Avant-Garde: The Case of Maya Deren.' *Cinema Journal. University of Texas Press.* 36 (2): 17–40.4 (Winter 1997).

4   See Maya Deren's discussion of servitors in *Divine Horsemen: The Living Gods of Haiti* (Document Text, McPhearson & Co, 1953; p. 71)

5   See 'Amateur versus Professional' in *Film Culture,* 1965.

6   See the documentary *In the Mirror of Maya Deren,* 'Im Spiegel der Maya Deren,' Directed by Martina Kudlácek, 2002.

7   *Maya Deren and the American Avant-Garde,* edited by Bill Nichols, is a collection of essays on Deren's work that focuses more on her poetics, ethics of form, aesthetic agency, dance, magic, and choreocinema than the oracular voice that comes through in her silent film (University of California Press, 2001).

8   See the collected works on film, *Essential Deren: Collected Writings on Film,* edited by Bruce R. McPhearson (Document Text, 2005) and *The Legend of Maya Deren, Vol 1 Part 1: Signatures (1917-1942)* by VeVe A. Clark, Millicent Hodson, and Catrina Neiman. (Anthology Film Archives, 1984).

9   See Laurencine Lot: *Carlotta Ikeda - La danse Buto et au-delà,* p. 70 (Favre, 2005).

Grace

'I had an abortion, that's how I dealt with it,' mother declared when I asked her about an incident. Mother had class. She had class because her integrity was always impeccable. Since integrity never goes out of fashion, her words still reverberate in my ears. About the same time when she instructed me to not have any children — as that would be the greatest realization in life — we had a talk about the love of her life before my father. They broke-up, suddenly, and to make sure that the break-up would stay that way and be quite irrevocable she did two things. She had an abortion first, and then she married my father not long after.

She was in love with an aviator who worked for the army. I can't remember how many years they were involved, but it may have been 5 years or so. They each had their own work and apartment, but the man ended up living with my mother. This being the early 60s, taking such liberties before marriage was considered quite advanced, speaking politely, for in reality, I doubt that many endorsed this lifestyle. The early 60s culture was not a kind culture to people who preferred their independence, while at the same time making a move towards co-habitation with no strings attached. At the personal level, I think that both my mother and her aviator lover were quite content with their lot, considering their love both serious and special. At least that was her unambiguous perception of it.

Now, why break up, if all things were clear? Mother told the following story: Her aviator lover had a colleague and good friend who experienced being pressured by his family to introduce my mother's lover to a woman, his cousin, in the village he was from. Now, why was this on the table at all, when the man was already in a relationship? Why would he be interested at all in meeting this other woman, when he practically already lived with one, something that his own friend was also painfully aware of? He wasn't interested. But then the culturally obsessed people weren't interested either in hearing that the man was *merely* in a relationship. All they needed to know was that the man was *not* married. As long as he was not married, he was thus on the market. Whatever other relationship he might have had, or was still having, was of no consequence as far as this family was concerned. So they insisted. They pressured their son to make the proper introductions between my mother's lover and this other woman.

Mother said no. She said no, when both men came to her and justified the awkward situation. They said: 'it's for the family, so they won't take offence. We'll only be gone 3 days, meet the woman, and then tell the family that there's no interest in pursuing this relation further.' Mother said no. 'Why is this necessary?' she wanted to know. 'Why is this necessary when we all know already that there's no interest?' Mother was not into wasted time and situations that were not straight.

As the two men also insisted, now claiming that the whole thing would be done in the interest of not losing face, it was my mother's turn to lose her interest. She simply said to her lover that unless he came up with a serious argument, she was not going to agree to the meeting of another woman for the prospect of marriage. She also made a promise right then and there: 'if you go, don't come back here.' The man went.

Upon his return he found all of his belongings neatly packed and placed outside the door. Mother had changed the lock too, so he couldn't enter. The man was stunned. He went out in the street and started calling her out. She came to the window and posed him a question: 'Did I or did I not say that if you go, you can't come back here?' He had to answer. As he did he made a mistake. 'Well, yeah,' he said, 'but this is ridiculous.' 'Ridiculous?' mother asked, and demanded an explanation. 'How is this ridiculous?' 'We're going out steady, live together, and we're going to have a family,' the man said, to which mother replied. 'I also thought so, just as I was about to tell you that I was pregnant.' 'That's wonderful,' the man yelled from the street. 'Let me in, won't you?' She replied: 'what makes you think that I'm still pregnant? I was three days ago, but I'm not anymore. While you were meeting another woman, I had an abortion.' Now the thunder, if you can imagine this scene. Mother asked me to imagine it too. I did. It was loud, and devastating. 'This is ridiculous,' the man said to mother again, crying. Mother said, 'this is the second time when you tell me that what I did is ridiculous, and I see that you're not prepared to produce an argument. Take your things and go. Reflect on your inability to see things clearly.'

Now, how is that for a story of a deathly resolve? Or was it saving grace? Mother was so strong, I always thought, and she stayed that way. Six months after this incident mother found my father, also a man in the army, and better at arguments — he was a mathematician. She married him on the spot. Meanwhile, however, the aviator kept coming to her place to plead with her. When he heard she got married, he made a last attempt. He came over to the apartment. He called out in the street again. Father came to the window. Then mother came to the window. The aviator said: 'I give you a month. If by any chance you regret having married this man, please come back to me.' Mother never did, though she confessed that there was an incident with my father in that month that gave her cause to regret having married him. But she decided not to leave him. She said that *that* would have been ridiculous. Not only ridiculous, but pathetic too. In a committed relationship, one is allowed to make a blunder. Father's offense was to say something very stupid to her. In my mother's practice of living life this meant getting ready to declare war. Mother was not good at tolerating stupid things, but if the person could argue and properly defend their stupidity, then they would get a chance. She would hear them out, and only then pass judgment. In our household we used to have logic debates. I like them a lot. I would also win a lot. My sister not so much. She was not given to much reflection. Defending a stubborn or stupid position didn't come easy to her. When my sister declared that mother should have just married the man she loved, in spite of what he did, mother was not kind to her when she couldn't argue for why that would have been a good idea.

As a small girl, I asked mother to tell me this story countless times. My sister only heard it once… I could never get enough of the level of awesomeness that I would find in every detail. I still can't get past the astonishment that mother would get herself an abortion, because the man she loved called her ridiculous. But I can see why such a thing deserves capital punishment. Calling another ridiculous without providing evidence for it is beyond excuse, as such an accusation carries a type of entitlement that's beyond redemption. If only people could hear themselves… So I asked mother to tell me this story countless times because of its images. There was no end to how I would imagine mother calling her doctor the minute the man stepped out of the house to do what she said he must not. Because there was no sound reason for it. I liked to imagine as well that while her lover would be on this trip to save his face, mother would be on her trip to the doctor's to save her grace. Every time I would imagine such details, I'd ask mother to corroborate my fantasy. I was never off the mark. You can imagine my excitement at being able to guess with such profound precision.

Or was the man interested in this other woman, and that's why he actually went? I asked mother about it. She said she didn't want to speculate, as this speculation would put her on an ugly track, where she would have to deem then man she loved insincere. 'Why would I do that?' she asked me, 'when I can't have evidence for it.' What she *did* consider was the unnecessary in the situation. For her the story was simple: it was not necessary for the man she lived with to go on a trip to meet another for the prospect of marriage. Not even in the interest of maintaining the goodwill of his friend. How would that act serve her? As to how this friend disrespected the already existing relationship, that was another territory she wasn't going to go to. She thought it was simply too dumb, and utterly pointless to waste time on what the other couldn't see as a matter of plain obviousness. And if he did see it, but pretended not to see it, then that was worse. She decided that whatever motivated the two men, her lover and his friend, with the consequence of cornering her for no apparent sound reason she could see, was not her story to tell. But she was sure of her capacity to act in accordance. Which she did.

So mother's break-up and ensuing abortion was due to the fact that her lover took her lightly. But the greatest mistake was to call her own true justice ridiculous. It was not ridiculous what she demanded, basically a properly constructed explanation, and it was not ridiculous when she had her abortion. In her head it was quite clear that since she was not interested in having a child all on her own, there was only one thing to do. The moralists would disagree, but since when is one's own true justice subject to moral issues?

Mother did what she needed to do right then and there in response to a situation that already begged itself to be impossible. What was mother to do, take it all in good stride and good humor? Because it was a joke, or because culture also has to win in intimate wars? She wasn't interested in going to war with culture and the stupid things that culture makes people say and do. She was interested in going to war with the one who was most precious to her. Win the dispute fair and square. But he abstained. He ran from the battlefield, and thought that he could just come back and re-engage with loving kindness.

I'm not sure what lesson I've learned myself from mother's story, but this I did learn: nothing can trump the straight story. Magicians and con men can try, but when the straight story is strong, all the tricks fall apart, the enchantment wearing off faster than the thinnest cloud transiting over the sky at high speed. A strong resolve is full of grace. It is also beyond regrets. In a way, I think that part of the pleasure I had in listening to mother's story here was also due to my desire to test her spine. Was she really that strong? Not if she showed any regrets. I wanted to catch her on this. I couldn't. Every time I thought I'd come close, she'd cut me off with some story of what she knew in actuality. Her story was straight because it was not based on emotion, fantasy, and projection. Hence, no matter how many traps I'd lay for her, or invent new clever tricks for a new turn of the wheel, she'd put me to shame. Bad magician...

I understand why mother said, 'never have children,' because the story that has children in it also has a father in it, who will always have a say in it. If the woman is lucky, the father's saying would be more than the sum of the ridiculous; it would be on a track of what we call decent human behavior. Mother liked to point out a fallacy. She'd say that most women tend to think of their children as theirs alone, invoking creation, gestation, and care, committing the mistake of taking the children's father lightly. She used to laugh at the concept of 'single mothers,' raising 'their' children.

After father died when I was eight and she never remarried, she became a single mother, but she resisted this label. 'Even dead, your father still has a say in it. We are all subject to his ghost,' she would say, and that would settle quite a few disputes. If an independent woman subjects herself to others having a say in it, as it were, it stands to reason that the very possibility of a relationship can be questioned. Who or what are we having them for, these relationships? I'm not taking sides here. I may never have gotten children by the grace of my mother's wisdom, but I've been in relationships that I cherish, and yet I think that if we must have a conversation about the value of self-reliance, which my mother was all in favor of and fought for with a martial arts spirit, then we have to go down the rabbit hole and ask the question of what the purpose of all of it is, that is to say, the purpose that's not already broadcast by societal indictments, ideology, or ideas of emancipation and empowerment in vogue.

I'm not sure what we all understand by all the concepts we surround ourselves with, live by, and believe in. Why is a childless woman considered a witch? – even now, not just in the past. One strategy of dealing with labels that are constitutive of negative or detrimental identities, so to speak, has been to reclaim them via a new framing. If it was shameful to be a childless witch in the past, now we must be proud of it. This tactic is efficient to a point, but because essentially it's nonsense, it goes nowhere. What has pride got to do with anything? Claiming and re-claiming power has only the function of inverting a hierarchy. It doesn't solve the problems with structural institutions. For all the work we do towards recognition, last I've checked most women are still dependent on men and their children, and most men still don't have any respect for women. Meanwhile we all yell, or lament pathetically, as our memory of lamentation as an art in itself is now completely forgotten.

I hear Carlotta Ikeda saying, 'jump,' only so she could see how you landed. Power is never located where you think. Sometimes it's nowhere other than the sole of your feet. Other times it sits in the timbre of your voice, or indeed, your silence. When Pasolini's Medea embodied by a mute singer appears on your screen, you want to heed attention to what power comes out of that presence. When you hear a drummer 'beat the loa into his head,' as the Vodouists have it, you'll see a quick displacement of power in the arrival of spirit in the material body. Power is also in the footprints you leave in the sand. Power is in settling scores. Your no is no, and your yes is yes. Gaining the clarity that goes into making distinctions requires conscious effort. Settling scores leaves you relaxed in your own perception of how power manifests. Not a thing for the lazy, who confuse stepping into a calm sea with permissions to 'just be yourself.' Who is this self, ironically always acting on the latest broadcasts? While the majority follows self-empowerment recipes shared in 'communities' that validate imported identities and imitations, the childless witch is relentless in asking true questions. These questions are simple, as their premise in anchored in curiosity, a thirst for discovery, and self-reliance: 'if I jump, how will I land?'

There are as yet endless questions that I want to pose myself, turn every label and every name inside out. But what would be the purpose of it? To show that language changes over time? To show that we develop reading skills that can re-frame these changes? That language is dynamic does not automatically imply that we can all read, that we can all find saving grace in shifting identities, or that we can all dance a dramatic dance?

What I'm interested in at all times is the writing on the wall. We can all see it, but can we also read it? I see the index finger of the childless witch pointing to the sacrificed eggs. It's a less bloody affair than when chickens are involved. But there's a roundness here, like that of a circle. A circle of magic for present times.

CPSIA information can be obtained
at www.ICGtesting.com
Printed in the USA
LVHW041307260321
682575LV00020B/297